D1200492

MEDIEVAL MINIATURES

# Medieval Miniatures

FROM THE DEPARTMENT OF MANUSCRIPTS

(FORMERLY THE "LIBRARY OF BURGUNDY")

THE ROYAL LIBRARY OF BELGIUM

COMMENTARIES BY L. M. J. DELAISSÉ

FOREWORD BY H. LIEBAERS

INTRODUCTION BY F. MASAI

HARRY N. ABRAMS, INC. PUBLISHERS NEW YORK

Library of Congress Catalog Card Number: 65-12094

Harry N. Abrams, Inc., New York
Printed and bound in West Germany

# CONTENTS

Page

FOREWORD 7

INTRODUCTION 9

THE MINIATURES

1. An Author at His Writing Desk (Ms. 18723, f. 17 v) 18
2. Faith Crushing the False Gods and Crowning the Martyrs (Ms. 10066–77, f. 115 v) 22
3. Title Page (Ms. 9188–89, f. 10 v)* 26
4. Christ Healing the Leper (Ms. 9428, f. 23) 30
5. The Evangelist Luke (Ms. 18383, f. 84 v)* 34
6. St. Gregory the Great and His Deacon Peter (Ms. 9916–17, f. 1 v)* 38
7. Christ Washing the Feet of the Apostles (Ms. 9222, f. 87 v) 42
8. The Nativity; The Evangelist Matthew (Ms. 10527, ff. 15 v and 16 r)* 46
9. Doubting Thomas (Ms. 10607, ff. 149 v and 150 r) 50
10. Psalter Page in Gold and Blue Letters (Ms. 9961–62, f. 74)* 54
11. The Nativity; The Annunciation to the Shepherds; The Adoration of the Magi (Ms. 9174, f. 27) 58
12. The Chamberlain of the King of Majorca (Ms. 9169, f. 52 v)* 62
13. The Crucifixion with the Virgin, St. John, and Donors (Ms. 9217, f. 115 v)* 66
14. Farming in a "Good Democracy" (Ms. 11201–2, f. 241) 70
15. Emperor Charles IV and the Seven Electors (Ms. 15652–56, f. 26)* 74
16. Charles V of France as Patron of the Sciences (Ms. 9505–6, f. 2 v) 78
17. Christ Enthroned Surrounded by the Symbols of the Four Evangelists (Ms. 9125, f. 178)* 82
18. The Circumcision (Ms. 10176–78, f. 222) 86

19–20. Jean de Berry Presented to the Madonna by His Two Patron Saints (Ms. 11060–61, ff. 10 and 11)* 90

21. The Creation and Fall of the Angels (Ms. 9001, f. 19) 96
22. The Madonna of the Crescent (Ms. 11035–37, f. 6 v)* 100
23. The Annunciation (Ms. 10767, f. 30) 104
24. Two Scenes from the Apocalypse (Ms. 9020–23, ff. 137 v and 138 v) 108
25. The Entombment (Ms. 21696, f. 50 v) 112
26. St. Augustine Reading His *City of God* (Ms. 9015, f. 1) 116
27. Simon Nockart Presenting the *Chroniques de Hainaut* to Philip the Good (Ms. 9242, f. 1)* 120
28. The Patriarch of India Approaching the Tomb of the Apostle Thomas (Ms. 9278–80, f. 45) 124
29. The Tree of Jesse (Ms. 9511, f. 15)* 128
30. René d'Anjou Watching the Mortification of Vain Pleasure (Ms. 10308, f. 76)* 132
31. The Punishment of the Rebellious Angels (Ms. 11063, f. 3) 136
32. The Dominican Brochard at Work (Ms. 9095, f. 1) 140
33. Scenes from the Life of the Virgin (Ms. 9231, f. 179) 144
34. Episodes in the Life of Charles V (Ms. 9232, f. 423)* 148
35. The Garden of Eden (Ms. 9047, f. 1 v) 152
36. King Godfrey of Denmark Giving Audience to the Four Envoys of Charlemagne (Ms. 9066, f. 169 v) 156
37. Christ Before Pilate (Ms. II 7619, f. 38 v) 160
38. The Crucifixion (Ms. 9215, f. 129)* 164
39. St. Waudru Arriving in Hibernia (Ms. 9243, f. 115) 168
40. Philip the Good Attending a Mass Sung by the Choir of Burgundy (Ms. 9092, f. 9) 172
41. David Aubert Presenting a Copy of *Cy nous dit* to Philip the Good (Ms. 9017, f. 38 v)* 176
42. The Emperor Anthony Victorious over the Saracens (Ms. 9967, f. 18) 180
43. Two Episodes from the *Romance of Girart of Nevers* (Ms. 9631, ff. 77 and 26 v) 184
44. The Entry into Jerusalem (Ms. 9081–82, f. 5) 188
45. Margaret of York at Prayer (Ms. 9272–76, f. 182)* 192
46. Margaret of York Practicing the Seven Acts of Mercy (Ms. 9296, f. 1) 196
47. Scipio Africanus Sending His Spies to the Numidian Camp (Ms. 10475, f. 8)* 200
48. St. Barbara (Ms. IV 40, ff. 17 v and 18 r) 204
49. The Apostles Peter and Andrew Answering the Call of Christ (Ms. 9008, f. 286) 208
50. The Crowning with Thorns (Ms. II 158, ff. 79 v and 80 r) 212

* Miniatures reproduced smaller than the original size; all others are full size

## FOREWORD

THIS BOOK will present in these fifty miniatures a vivid picture of the manuscript collections in which the Royal Library of Belgium in Brussels so rightly prides itself. The commentator had to select the miniatures as well as prepare their annotation – a task which resulted in continuous interrelated and stimulating problems. Some of the miniatures chosen are well known; two or three have been frequently reproduced in the past and their presence here should not be surprising. Their quality is so exceptional that even the specialists will not tire of seeing them.

Contained in this volume are also the best examples of the multiple aspects of illumination. They illustrate refinements of style, subjects that are ever changing, technical skills, richnesses of composition, as well as innovations in the layout of the page. An account is also provided of the inexhaustible wealth of marginal decorations, where the characteristics of a workshop can be recognized and the individual temperaments of the artists find free expression. At first glance, the miniatures reproduced here will seem rather disparate. Yet their composite image mirrors the infinite variety of the perceptive world that is hidden within the pages of the manuscripts.

In a few cases the selection was guided by personal interests. The choice of a certain book of hours, for instance, was dictated by the pride felt by the Royal Library in its recent acquisition.

The author also gave rein to his personal preferences. But the wealth of the treasures from which these fifty plates were gathered is so abundant that the liberty taken in the selection has not been detrimental to the beauty of the pieces presented.

Even though these reproductions speak for themselves, they cannot dispense with an explanatory text. Every illuminated page poses many questions to its viewer. The commentary accompanying the plates answers some of the most important queries. It would be impossible to retrace in detail the often extremely complicated history of each book. The author, keeping only to the essentials, has in no case failed to show the place occupied by the miniature in the book of which it is an integral part.

Miniatures lend themselves particularly well to color reproduction. These pictures, by the very nature of the books containing them, have been well preserved from the injurious effects of light, with the result that the colors have retained their original freshness.

A second advantage enjoyed by miniatures is that they can for the most part be reproduced in their actual size; the dimensions here have mostly the identical format of the original document.

However, color reproduction must still resolve a particularly arduous technical problem: that of rendering gold, and, above all, its relief. On this point, the desired perfection has not yet been achieved.

The reader can easily imagine what intensive research this volume has demanded on the part of the librarians and engravers. This book owes a great deal to their harmonious collaboration.

The Royal Library of Belgium was able to produce this book thanks to the initiative and active support of the *Banque de Paris et des Pays-Bas.* The introduction is by F. Masai, curator of the Department of Manuscripts. The choice of miniatures and the commentary are the work of L. M. J. Delaissé, assistant curator. May these few pictures be the faithful witnesses of the treasures accumulated throughout the centuries in the national collection of Belgium.

Herman Liebaers
Librarian

# INTRODUCTION

THE CULTIVATED PUBLIC has never had access to miniatures in the same way it has to other artistic wonders. The principal reason for keeping them so hidden from view is not their diminutive size – many pictures in our museums are no larger. It is that the fragility of the miniatures necessitates their being kept away from light and air and, consequently, from view. But we may be sure that the progress made in the techniques of conservation will shortly allow longer periods of exposure, if not permanent exhibition. Even so, most of these precious examples of medieval painting will remain hidden, for one can only really get to know books by turning their pages.

Yet, because of the great strides which have been made in color reproduction, miniatures can become accessible to all. In principle, from now on, every miniature can be reproduced. What horizons for the history of art!

By studying the miniatures in manuscripts one is able to extend back the history of Occidental painting by a thousand years. Thanks to them, the diversity and evolution of taste during the Gothic period may be known down to the smallest detail. The Romanesque period is hardly less accessible, with the numerous Bibles, lectionaries, missals and other books of the eleventh and twelfth centuries. Great numbers of miniatures of the Carolingian period are preserved, and even as far back as the Merovingian period, art may be studied in the illumination of books.

How many churches, abbeys, and palaces have forever disappeared, of which all that now remains is a manuscript. We have only to examine them to learn about the taste and wealth of the patrons who ordered or assembled these books. Despite this wealth of material, however, too few archaeologists and historians have ventured into the vast domain of book painting.

Throughout the ages, man has loved to illustrate and decorate his books. In the Egypt of the Pharaohs the *Book of the Dead* was admirably decorated with miniatures. Some fragments of parchment and papyrus show that the Greeks and Romans also knew and appreciated the decorated manuscript; but in classical antiquity, as in all major epochs of intense intellectual creativity, the book was considered to be primarily a means of conveying thought. Gradually, however, the other aspect of the book emerges and finally supersedes the latter, as books receive more special care and attention. When this occurs the book gains in value as an object – an object of ornamentation or of a cult – and loses, to some degree, its position as a message-bearer.

During the later Roman Empire this evolution of a book into an object of special notice is more pronounced because of the religious revolution of the time. Influenced by the reverence for texts in Oriental religions, greater care was taken in the copying, decoration, and binding. Gospels and Bibles became more and more sumptuous, despite protestations from the most intellectual among the Fathers of the Church and from those who advocated evangelical simplicity. Not only the texts were given special attention; the binding boards, too, were enriched by the work of sculptors in ivory or by artisans in gold and silver.

This development of books as objects of a cult or as ornaments obliges the historian to make a clear distinction between actual illustration and decoration. The understanding of certain texts throughout the ages has required explanatory figures, particularly in the treatises on science. On the other hand, the decoration of books, as opposed to their illustration, has no other aim than embellishment. The decoration of books often makes them more valuable and, in the case of holy books, renders them still more worthy of veneration.

The books of antiquity were illustrated for functional purposes; the art of decoration was hardly developed for its own sake. The books of the Middle Ages, on the contrary, were highly decorated. The history of the initial clearly demonstrates the difference between antique and medieval books.

The reader of a scientific work needs to locate the text he is studying without difficulty. The Greek and Roman scribes developed a system that enlarged the titles and initials as a practical aid to the reader. These titles, initials, or first words of the text retained their normal shape; only their size increased. No distinction was even made between majuscules and miniscules.

In Italy at the end of the fourth century, initials begin first to receive some decoration. Certain scribes added a small pen-stroke to an uncial *a*, giving it the appearance of a fish. Their imaginative power to ornament the initials was encouraged and colors were also introduced.

North of the Alps a great interest in the decorated initial was taken up by the barbaric peoples. The scribes' unbridled imaginations turned to effecting greatly elaborated initials.

Merovingian scribes broadened and lengthened the initials. They introduced décor inspired by fauna and flora to all the letters of certain titles. They painted the characters in many bright colors – red, green, or violet. In the British Isles the decoration became even more elaborate. An ecclesiastical center in Northumbria introduced into the decoration of initials ornaments that had the style and value of native jewels. It seems that in the more luxurious Gospel books the decoration not only of the binding but also of the beginning of the texts was entrusted to the most skilled among the metal workers. Thus were born those masterpieces of the medieval book, works universally known: the Books of Lindisfarne, of Kells, and of Lichfield.

In one century the medieval book had supplanted the book of antiquity. The modestly ornamented initial of fourth-century Italy had become the wonderful *letrine* initial demanding large sheets of parchment. Where all the refinements and wizardry of barbaric ornamentation were given full rein the *incipit* – especially of the Gospel texts – occupied an entire page.

The Carolingian Revival marked a return to classical sobriety and to illustration as such. It restored a taste for purely calligraphical beauty. However, precious books of the ninth century without vestiges of barbaric exuberance are rare. But if for a while the initial gave way to the rules of classical discipline, it was to blossom forth again without restrictions in the Romanesque period.

In the eleventh and twelfth centuries illumination became real figurative decoration. Miniaturists added human figures in their initials as well as the established barbaric ornaments, flowers, and animals. Veritable scenes came to be contained in the initials. The text naturally brought pressure to bear on the ornamentist by inspiring figurative decoration which thus became real illustration. Bonds were forged once more between the text and the picture; the initial itself at once lost much favor.

During the Gothic period the initial in the luxury book again enjoyed a certain importance. Gradually it regained a large part of the page by pushing diverse prolongations and elaborations into the margins. However, the initial never again obtained a position of absolute supremacy in the illuminated book. In fact, after the twelfth century illustration as such is the predominant characteristic of book illustration.

What has just been said about the initial is enough to point out that the period of its greatest proliferation coincided with the decline of illustration.

Book illustration was practically nonexistent in western Europe during the seventh and eighth centuries. It may be that the victory of the iconoclasts in Byzantium is partly responsible for the disappearance of illustrated books. Nonetheless, the picture reappeared in the Carolingian Revival, particularly with the genial drawings of the Utrecht Psalter. For centuries these drawings were a source of inspiration for illustrators in the British Isles. Above all, the manuscripts of Prudentius reintroduce us to the illustrated book (plate 2).

Illustrated Gospels were created in the churches and abbeys of southern Germany in the Ottonian era, the most brilliant time in their history. The portrait of the author as the frontispiece of a sacred text had been in familiar use since the end of antiquity (plate 1). A transcription of Gospel stories into pictures appears in the lectionaries of the Mass during the eleventh century. The legends of the saints were also favored with the same treatment. The book of evangelical pericopes and the *Dialogues* of St. Gregory the Great, in the Royal Library of Brussels, are perfect examples of the new character of these books (plates 4 & 6). They also demonstrate what summits were rapidly attained by the re-establishment of the illustrated book.

During the Gothic and Renaissance periods illustration spread to all sorts of literature. In these times of the progressive secularization of society and culture, art became transferred to the service of profane works as well as to the cult of God and the saints. The miniaturists were not obliged to satisfy a taste for luxury and fleeting fashions. They decorate chronicles, romances, and even treatises on hunting. The illustration and decoration of these books finally surpassed, in quality and number, what the ecclesiastical patrons, notably the abbots, could still create in their liturgical manuscripts. The books of hours themselves take on a worldly quality by their opulence and ostentation.

A great increase in the love of books at the end of the Middle Ages vigorously stimulated the art of illumination. In the principal centers, notably Paris, workshops were installed for decorating and illustrating books that were in incessant demand by an increasingly avid lay upper-class society. The number of illustrated manuscripts produced in France, Flanders, Italy, and all over western Europe is inconceivable. What is perhaps still more surprising is the creative imagination of this epoch, that was able to express pictorially so many texts that had never before been illustrated.

In the Gothic period the artisans of luxury books were usually laymen. We are infinitely less informed about the standing of the miniaturists during the preceding centuries. There are many indications, however, which seem to show that a lay element always played an important role in the decoration of books, at least in the miniatures of high quality. But it is quite evident that before the age when lay commissions became general an artist could not live only by decorating books. The monasteries supplied their own needs in the domain of books as in other areas. Only occasionally did they need a hand more skilled than one of their own scriptorium copyists. Once or twice in a century an abbey or an important church felt the need of a book of great richness.

From the Gothic period onward a layman could consider devoting himself to the illustration of books; during the preceding centuries a professional artist could only occasionally give time to illuminating. From this perhaps stems the considerable difference in originality between the miniatures of the earlier and later Middle Ages. The Gothic miniature vibrates with life and develops rapidly from within itself, whereas the miniature of the preceding centuries seems to be a transposition from an other art. Generally speaking, works in metal and ivory have left many traces of their influence on the miniature of the early Middle Ages. We have spoken of barbaric jewelry introduced into sacred books in the eighth century in England. Likewise, at Reichenau and at Echternach in the eleventh century contemporary frescoes inspired the illustrators of the Gospel stories. In other centers the transpositions from enamels are striking, as at Limoges, for example, or in the Meuse area. Even at the beginning of the Gothic period, the influence of a medium alien to book illustration can still be clearly seen. Many miniatures and decorated initials of the thirteenth century are no more than the transposition of a stained-glass window onto parchment!

Book painting rapidly evolved once it was established as an independent art. Not only did fashions change, bringing alternations and revolutions in coloring, for example, but even the resources of the art altered. The grace, the impulsive zest of the thirteenth-century draftsmen must not prevent us from recognizing the contribution made by their successors. Certain technical achievements reached their summit in the fourteenth century. In the fifteenth century a profound study of realism produced the portrait and a more realistic rendering of life, its emotions, its tragedy, its humor, and even its ugliness. In the conquest of perspective, the miniaturists of Flanders created those exquisite landscapes, full of depth and atmosphere, that constitute one of the virtues and one of the greatest charms of Flemish painting.

In his commentary L. Delaissé emphasizes the progress and, too, the weaknesses of Gothic illumination throughout the three centuries of its evolution. He insists particularly on the amazing contribution of the miniaturists, especially those of the fifteenth century, to the discovery of new values and the enrichment of Occidental sensibility.

The miniature faithfully reflects for us a millenary of Western civilization, through the variety and the inspiration of its techniques. The whole history of a region is mirrored in the collections of miniatures that were formed and enlarged there over the centuries. Such is the case of the "Library of Burgundy" in Brussels.

Unlike many public and private collections, the Royal Library of Belgium does not owe its existence to a sudden and recent prosperity. It was created by centuries of interest and patronage.

In 1559, Philip II sent for all his books from his subject countries and assembled them in Brussels, forming the first royal library. But it was a much larger patrimony that he regrouped. For centuries local princes and lords had shown their enlightened taste in collecting luxury books. The treasure of the province of Hainaut included illuminated manuscripts, and Louis de Male, the last count of Flanders, had acquired for his chapel the most beautiful liturgical books that the fourteenth-century native illuminators were capable of producing. With the marriage of Margaret de Male and Philip the Bold these books became part of the Burgundian appanage. Like all members of the House of Valois, the dukes of Burgundy were eminent book lovers. They seized every opportunity to acquire valuable manuscripts, and they all took pains to have books written and illuminated for themselves. Princes and courtiers used their masters' passion for fine books to their own advantage: they often sought the favor of dukes by offering them an illuminated manuscript (plate 39). Sometimes the vassals and favorites of the dukes even rivaled their masters – above all, Chevrot, Fillastre, and the Croys gave themselves with passion to the cult of illuminated books.

Little by little admirable pieces found their way in from France (plates 14, 16, 17, 19, 20, and 23), from England (plate 10), and from the Mediterranean countries (plate 12). These took their place in the "Library of Burgundy" beside the works of the best illuminators of the country: Jean Le Tavernier of Audernarde, Loyset Liédet, Simon Marmion, and others.

The library instituted in 1559 did not assemble all the books that had belonged to Burgundian dukes, duchesses, and their descendants. It did represent an important part of their collection, however, as is proved by the many marks of ownership in manuscripts belonging to Philip the Good, Charles the Bold, Margaret of York, or Anthony *le Grand Bâtard*. It is not without reason hat this royal collection of manuscripts was called the "Library of Burgundy."

However, all the manuscripts did not come from this source. Margaret of Austria's manuscripts and those of her ward, Charles V, joined many other Burgundian manuscripts in the King's collection, and there were many other works of different origins which came with them. Margaret of Valois, widow of Emmanuel Philibert, duke of Savoy, brought many precious books from Savoy to the library in Brussels; in many of the books one finds notes written in her hand. This enlightened princess also had bought one of the most beautiful private collections in Flanders: *78 volumes escriptes en parchemin et à la main* that belonged to Charles of Croy, prince of Chimay. Mary of Hungary, who had possessed the collection of the *Gouvernante* before bequeathing it to her nephew Philip II, had in her turn enriched it with pieces from abroad. It is to her that we owe one of the pearls of the collection, the Missal of Mathias Corvinus, king of Hungary (plate 49).

Since it originated under such circumstances it is not surprising that the Royal Library of

Brussels' possessions constitute one of the richest and most representative collections of painted manuscripts extant today. It is unrivaled for its miniatures of the Gothic period in the Low Countries. And the monuments it possesses of French, English, and even Italian illumination may be envied by the most celebrated museums and libraries.

The "Library of Burgundy" had nothing to show for the centuries preceding the Gothic period. However, the anticlericism of the eighteenth century filled this gap. The works brought in from the suppressed convents constitute this hoped-for complement to the Royal Library.

Some of the most beautiful books executed in Flanders or in the Meuse country during the eleventh and twelfth centuries had been preserved mainly by the Benedictine monasteries. All, unfortunately, did not come into the state collections; several of the most beautiful are the pride of foreign libraries. The greater part of the manuscripts, though, have been repatriated by our predecessors, particularly Father Van den Gheyn. He was responsible for the repurchase of hundreds of Belgian manuscripts which were incorporated into the royal collection in the nineteenth century.

Since the "Library of Burgundy" became the Department of Manuscripts of the Royal Library in Brussels, its collections have profited by an increased solicitude on the part of the public powers. It was possible to buy back a considerable number of manuscripts which had been dispersed from abbeys after the French Revolution. Many other acquisitions have been made since the institution of the present Royal Library in 1937. The first acquisition was the purchase of Charles van Hulthem's library, which added more than a thousand manuscripts to the state collection. Some of these books are very precious for the study of the history of Flemish art and the history of Dutch letters. During the last century the Royal Library was able to procure some fine pieces, sometimes veritable masterpieces of national and foreign illumination, such as the Carolingian Xanten Gospels (plate 1), the Hours of Hennessy (plate 50), the Hours of Mary van Vronensteyn (plate 37), and the Hours of Philip of Cleves (plate 48).

A much-needed inventory for these accumulated treasures was the undertaking of Frédéric Lyna. At first with the help of Camille Gaspar, then alone, this curator indefatigably listed and described hundreds of illuminated manuscripts. Guided by the surest instinct, Lyna was able to discover and evaluate the principal masterpieces of the collection. Some of his attributions are of the greatest importance for the history of Flemish art. A scholar as modest as he is enthusiastic, Lyna inspired the continuation of this important work. The commentaries by L. Delaissé on the miniatures reproduced here will help to explain the direction taken by present-day research.

Understanding and aesthetic enjoyment remain the supreme objectives in perusing manuscripts. Yet, art criticism is important, too. One must constantly try to sift and sort the merits of the artists and their works, to compare them, to oppose and to group them.

In a book of this kind it is undesirable to discuss the controversies concerning the attribution, dating, and localization of certain manuscripts because the commentaries present works of art that are rather new even to the cultivated public. Besides, such an undertaking would require far more space than could be given here. The author, therefore, limits himself to a simple analysis of the chosen subject. L. Delaissé has taken into account the most recent discoveries. He has pointed out the numerous problems encountered by the historian of illumination, aiming at opening new horizons and reviving interest in subjects apparently exhausted.

In a book of this type, destined for the general public, there is no bibliography of the numerous subjects treated. The catalogues of the Department of Manuscripts at the Royal Library, particularly the works of F. Lyna, will furnish necessary references for specialists and persons interested in more thorough information.

The essential aim of this book is to make known and to offer for appreciation some of the most beautiful miniatures of the "Library of Burgundy," so that they may be esteemed not only for their intrinsic value and beauty, but also for their historical significance.

François Masai
Curator of Manuscripts

# THE MINIATURES

1

# An Author at His Writing Desk

XANTEN GOSPEL LECTIONARY. *Miniature dating perhaps from the Roman period, fourth century; added to a manuscript from the Palace School, ninth century.*
*221 folios ($10^1/_4 \times 8^5/_8$"); 12 illuminated canon tables; 2 full-page miniatures.*
*Ms. 18723, f. 17 v*

IN ORDER TO understand this miniature painted on a purple ground and to place it in the history of miniature painting, the book to which the miniature belongs must be described. One must decide whether the purple folio is a genuine Roman painting or a product of the Carolingian Revival. As we shall see, to ascribe it to any of the centuries between these two epochs is hardly worth considering. The manuscript comprises the Four Gospels, a type of book often found in the early centuries, when full copies of the New Testament were rare and copies of the Bible almost nonexistent. In manuscripts of this kind the Gospels are, according to custom, preceded by Eusebian canons, that is to say, by a table of concordance which enables one to find parallel passages in any of the Gospels. These canon tables are decorated; they are transcribed under majestic porticos, the classical character of which appears in the Roman arches surmounting the columns and in the marble used for the buildings, a material which was seldom represented in the Middle Ages. From the stylistic point of view another detail also reveals the classical model: the shadows thrown by the columns. We shall have to wait for the fifteenth century before the western European artist again observes and paints this natural phenomenon.

The Gospels are written in the minute type of handwriting called Carolingian miniscule, a style developed during the reign of Charlemagne; its simple and rounded form was inspired by

the script of antiquity. The headings, written in Roman capitals, attest to this survival of the more remote civilization. In fact, the manuscript shows no trace of the intermediate period during which a new world was laboriously striving to rebuild the culture it had itself destroyed.

Originally, the manuscript, to which this isolated miniature on a purple ground was added, contained only one full-page miniature, not the four – one for each Gospel – we generally find in this type of book. Here the four sacred authors are assembled in a single page and surmounted by a Christ in glory. The painting is badly damaged: it seems that the pigment was not adhesive enough for the parchment, or that the latter did not receive adequate treatment before color was applied. In any case, the years and perhaps the constant handling it has had have brought it to its present condition. A closer inspection reveals work of a classic beauty such as will not be found again until the fifteenth century. As for the evangelists, they are perhaps the last of this quality we shall see of the Roman type in the Western world. On an extremely small surface, with a few strokes of his brush, the artist has painted the four seated authors, with their symbols above them: the bull, the eagle, the lion, and the angel. The subjects are painted with such a sense of volume, such natural postures and beauty of line, particularly in the folds of the togas, that they could not fail to satisfy even the most stern critics. It is scarcely conceivable that one of these miniaturists who, only a few years before, had been content with the clumsy geometrical patterns of the Merovingians or the intricate stylization inspired by insular miniature painting, could have suddenly adopted such a noble style. The execution of such a masterpiece implies the presence of artists from Byzantium or from southern Italy, where the Roman tradition still survived. This one beautiful page, highly influenced by classic art, suffices to illustrate these Gospels, long in use at St. Victor of Xanten and acquired by the Royal Library in the nineteenth century.

How, then, shall we account for the presence in a liturgical book of the folio reproduced here, since it was not included in the original quire but is merely an addition? To answer this question we must be quite sure we know the subject of the miniature. This purple folio represents a person writing on a manuscript which lies on a lectern. It is impossible to see how the writer holds his pen because the pigment has cracked at that very place; it seems, however, that it was held between thumb and forefinger. The writing desk is not exactly in front of the scribe, but slightly out of axis, and the book is visible to those who are looking at the miniature. This was probably intentional but it may also be a weakness in perspective, since this page shows other defects of the same kind: there is some heaviness about the shoulders, and the left knee protrudes beyond the right. And yet what a natural attitude, what individuality in this face of indubitably Roman character with such hair, and the straight high-bridged nose continuing the line of the forehead!

Who is this person? Undoubtedly an author, for in those early days the work of a scribe was not considered a worthy subject for a picture. Moreover, he is a profane author, for otherwise he would have a halo. We even wonder why he was not provided at a later stage with a nimbus. Two slight notches in the parchment on either side of the shoulders might suggest that someone tried to draw an aura by means of a stylet fixed on a compass, but the marks may be due to tiny accidents in the parchment as there are many others on this page. Why should this tentative tracing of a halo never have been completed? The rare cases in which the author is represented without a halo are all very close in style to this miniature on a purple background; the other folio of the Xanten Gospels, in which the four evangelists have no halo, is the most important example. This last picture, however, as well as two or three others we know, are of an entirely medieval conception and the frame in which they are set is the sign of their subordination to the manuscript they illustrate. The subject of the purple folio, on the contrary, is an independent representation complete in itself; it discloses, on the part of the artist, the spirit of antique art. Thus this painting could hardly have been made after the fifth century; it is truly Roman, not yet Byzantine. Probably from sheer respect for its great age the artists preserved this folio after having drawn their inspiration from it. This page, indeed, has been used as a model for the miniature containing the four evangelists: we find the same human type in both paintings. On the other hand, from a technical point of view these two miniatures are completely different. This purple page is not just painted, like the other, but colored with a purple dye; the pigment, moreover, is a kind of bright enamel, much thicker than the unsubstantial gouache which is applied on a white background. A last detail: a double line made with a stylet frames the subject. This frame was certainly added later on, rather carelessly too, for the reason that the miniature, however realistic, was unacceptable if it could not be fixed in space by some device. The frame is so poorly made that we cannot hold the illuminator of the page with the four evangelists responsible for this modification. On his part such an alteration would be equivalent to vandalism. All this shows that the medieval artist could not appreciate a human representation at once so realistic and so abstract. The imitators had copied this folio's details but they had not grasped its spirit.

The controversy aroused by this exciting subject is certainly not over. At any rate, it is more difficult to prove that this purple folio was executed during the Carolingian epoch than to admit its Roman origin. In any case, such a miniature remains one of the greatest pages in the history of miniature painting.

## 2 Faith Crushing the False Gods and Crowning the Martyrs

PRUDENTIUS, Psychomachia *and other texts, including the* Physiologus de naturis animalium et bestiarum, *in Latin. Former Lotharingia. Tenth century.*
*164 folios ($10^1/_4 \times 6^7/_8$"); 47 pen drawings in the text, slightly touched up with color.*
*Ms. 10066–77, f. 115 v*

NOT EVEN intentionally could one succeed in illustrating a happier contrast than that between the first two miniatures reproduced in this book. After the presentation of a purely classical subject painted on such elaborate material as purple parchment, here is a rather neglected page decorated with rudimentary but vigorous sketches. Apart from the geometrical patterns or the stylized animals of the Merovingian period, these drawings are the first manifestation in Gaul of an art which is truly local, even though necessarily inspired by the models of antiquity. Furthermore, the *Psychomachia* of Prudentius can be placed among the first texts of which the decoration could be labelled an "illustration." For this reason it is indispensable to say a few words about the work itself before describing the two pictures selected.

Aurelius Clemens Prudentius is the first poet of the Christian world. Born in Spain, probably at Calahorra, in 348, he had been extremely well educated. He became a lawyer, entered the public service and even reached an important position under Theodosius. At the age of fifty-seven, he decided to retire into a monastery where he died shortly after, in about 410. Before adopting the religious life, he arranged a sort of complete edition of his works and wrote in the foreword a short autobiography from which the above-mentioned facts are taken.

Prudentius' literary production was almost entirely polemical. He made a direct attack on

Ecce lacescentem collatis uirib; audet
Prima ferire fidem ueteru cultura deor;

Illa hostile caput falerataq; tẽpora uittis
Altior insurgens labefactat & ora cruore
De pecudum satiata solo applicat & pede calcat.
Elisos in mortem oculos animamq; malignã
Fracta intercepti comertia gutturis artant
Difficilemq; obitum suspiria longa fatigant

imperial Roman religion, stigmatizing the moral frailties of its gods; he fought the heresies that infested the Church at the time, especially those denying the divinity of Christ, and he sang the praise of the martyrs, chiefly those of the Spanish Church. Lastly, in another vein, he composed hymns of unsophisticated symbolism and even wrote out a description of 49 pictures, probably frescoes intended for a basilica. All of his works have the especial character of an apologetic. Prudentius' *Psychomachia* describes the struggle between Christian virtues and pagan vices. The literary merits of this poem are rather negligible; it was, however, the most read and the most copied of Prudentius' works. His success in the Carolingian period might seem surprising were it not that the Holy Roman Empire at that time was still crammed with non-Christian elements. Christianity did not penetrate into all classes of society until the Romanesque period.

In the upper part of this page, Faith, with a halo, is threatened by a warrior armed with an ax. In response to this menace, Faith assumes a very dignified attitude; it seems as if she could restrain her assailant simply by a gesture of her hands. But a contest cannot be avoided and the two enemies are set one against the other. The "false god" has just fallen to the ground but tries to get up, still fighting. The gesture of defense is particularly well observed. Faith wins, of course; she tramples down her enemy under her foot and knee.

The drawing at the bottom of the page represents Faith again, this time after the victory. She is standing on the dead body of her heathen opponent and crowns the martyrs. We notice that the artist has not drawn the legs of the two yet-uncrowned martyrs standing in the rear. The ground is drawn as if it were plowed with furrows and hillocks; a vine tree has been painted on the far right to help fill in this rather sketchy picture.

The eloquence of these pictures is so evident that it hardly needs mentioning. The gesture of Faith which seems to disarm her enemy, the attitude of the figure in the center on the point of striking with his ax, the wrestling of the two adversaries – these actions are rendered in the first picture with great intensity. The second picture is not quite so vigorous; the attitudes are more restrained, although an exception should be made for Faith. The way her arms are crossed remains a mystery; some detail that gave this gesture its significance must have been omitted by an illuminator who has not understood his model.

On the other hand, the shortcomings and the awkwardnesses of the drawings are quite as apparent as their good qualities. In his terror the fallen man opens enormous hands and his right foot seems to have been entirely omitted by the painter. The feet of Faith, victorious over false religion, are twisted in the most incredible way; one is even under the impression that the artist has drawn the right foot twice. The hands and feet are generally exaggerated, either large or much too small. The faces are very sketchy; they do not lack life, however, thanks to the firmness of the pen drawings.

In spite of its weak points this page and many of the drawings in the manuscript have such a definite style that they are evidently inspired by models of exceptional quality, however distant these may be. If we study a few other illustrated manuscripts of Prudentius, we reach the conclusion that they derive from one of several copies dating back to the early period. The architecture, some sketches of groups, and some bold foreshortenings are unthinkable if we do not admit this origin. We are well aware, besides, of the deep and lasting influence of the famous Utrecht Psalter on this illumination and even on Carolingian art in general. The masterly drawings contained in the Psalter, the grandiose and almost visionary movements condensed into countless little pictures, the breath of life that pervades the illustration of the text, all this is traceable in some of the copies of Prudentius, among them this Brussels manuscript. This copy dates back to the tenth century and for want of more precise data, ancient Lotharingia has been suggested for its location.

If one looks again at the miniature reproduced here, forgetting some unfortunate blemishes, one can better appreciate the superb attitude of the warrior wielding his ax as well as the beauty of the folds of his garments, the overwhelming dignity of Faith, and the power of her gesture. Likewise, if one carefully analyzes the entwined and wrestling bodies, one is dumfounded by the temerity of the artist. Such spontaneous and intense movement was probably the result of a reaction, presumably unconscious, against the tyrannical formalism of the soon-degenerate Carolingian Revival. This spirit of reaction, if it could have been maintained, would have given birth to masterpieces; in fact it died away, to be found again, but more restrained, in the Gothic period, of which it was the distant forerunner.

## 3 Title Page

ST. WOLBODON'S PSALTER. *Trier or perhaps Utrecht. About 1000.*
*236 folios (12 1/4 × 9"); several very large initials in gold.*
*Ms. 9188–89, f. 10 v*

THIS PSALTER is a book of primarily liturgical character. It differs from the biblical psalter, which also contains the hundred and fifty psalms attributed to David, but simply presents them as one among the other books of the Old Testament. It also differs from that particular type of psalter which comes into fashion in the thirteenth and fourteenth centuries as a prayer book destined primarily for the laity, but only to be replaced still later by the book of hours. We will soon encounter two very luxurious examples of these devotional books: the Psalter of Guy de Dampierre, count of Flanders (plate 9), and that of Godfrey of Croyland, abbot of Peterborough (plate 10). But the manuscript from which comes the page presented here contains a psalter which is different again from the common liturgical psalter. This one was meant for the different hours of the office on each day of the week. It follows the sequence of the liturgical recitation of psalms established by St. Benedict, not the order in the Bible. The Brussels manuscript, and a few others, belong to a special category of psalters in which we may witness the primitive Latin liturgy. At the end of the antique period, the office consisted of reading a series of psalms in biblical order, each of them being followed with a recitation by the celebrant of a prayer called a collect. Thus the name Psalter with Collects is given to this rare kind of book.

B
EA
TVS
VIR
QVI
NON
ABIIT
INCON

Each of the three parts of the Psalter begins with a decorated page comprising a large gold initial touched up with a little color and followed by other smaller letters, also written in gold. In this page appear the opening words of the first psalm, reading: *Beatus vir qui non abiit in con*. . . . The last word is left unfinished and terminates in ordinary letters on the next page: . . . *silio impiorum*. . . . In the top margin, between the second and the third letter, we notice an odd sign written with red ink. It is a neum, that is, one of the first musical notations used in the Middle Ages; it is put here as a reminder of a marginal gloss concerning the word *Beatus*. The scribe showed his originality by using for reference symbols the neums he must have learned in order to copy music.

In the Northumbrian manuscripts the decorative system established by the Merovingians, which consisted of writing on a large scale and ornamenting the first letters of the text, received true embellishment for the first time. The process was adopted during the Carolingian period, somewhat varied and without insular decorative motifs, in a first-rate manuscript: the Sacramentary of Drogo, executed between 826 and 855 (Paris, Bibliothèque Nationale, Ms. lat. 9428). The decorative conception of the three pages of the Wolbodon Psalter belongs to this tradition in its Carolingian form but with traces of the insular interlace pattern which had come via St. Gall or Echternach. It is, besides, to the latter center that we should relate our manuscript, particularly for the style of writing.

The Psalter once belonged to Wolbodon who was *écolâtre* (in charge of the episcopal school) in Utrecht and afterward Bishop of Liège from 1018 to 1021. This fact is attested by Renier, chronicler and Benedictine monk of the Abbey of St. Lawrence in Liège. In his *Life of St. Wolbodon* he declares that the psalter of the holy bishop was preserved in the library of his monastery. Legend grew from this remark and transformed the book that had belonged to the sainted protector of the abbey into a manuscript which, so the story goes, he composed and wrote with his own hand. Modern critics are more cautious: the liturgists know that these collects date back to the first centuries of the Christian Church and palaeographers have traced several different handwritings in the same codex.

Wolbodon could have had this manuscript made only before his ascent to the episcopal throne of Liège (1018). Indeed, at the beginning of the Psalter are litanies which mention the saints who were not the object of special worship in Liège, but in Utrecht: St. Martin, the patron of the cathedral, SS. Boniface, Willibrord, and Pontian. However, we also find there the names of many saints whose worship is localized in Trier; these names come after that of St. Paulinus, protector of Trier. This is not surprising when one knows the relationship of the bishopric of Utrecht to Echternach, a foundation of St. Willibrord in the diocese of Trier, and to Trier itself at the end of the tenth century, under the glorious episcopate of Egbert, a prelate of Dutch origin. The spiritual radiation from Trier to the monasteries in the region manifests itself in a material way in the books written there, between the eighth and the eleventh century, for other churches in the Empire (plate 4). Thus the contents of the manuscript confirm our previous remarks concerning its style, which had already led us to think of Trier as the probable center of its execution.

The various series of saints' names, grouped in the litanies in successive layers depending on the places where they were worshiped – Trier, then Utrecht – attest at least to a spiritual relationship between these two centers. The liturgical calendars often found in those books are, of course, made up in the same way. They include, therefore, not only the specific devotions of the places for which they were made but also of the typical cults in the first centers of religious life on which these new seats were dependent. We realize that a thorough study of the litanies and calendars is indispensable to the history of these epochs.

This Psalter for the use of the bishopric of Utrecht, kept in Liège as early as the thirteenth century, seems then to have been made at the time Wolbodon was still an *écolâtre*. It remains to be seen whether a book of such quality could possibly have been made in Trier, and not in Utrecht in the style of Trier. This question is the more delicate since no manuscript has yet been found that was, for certain, made in Utrecht at this time. It is generally agreed that the Psalter was written in the years around 1000, and before 1018, when Wolbodon was elected to the bishopric of Liège.

4

# Christ Healing the Leper

ECHTERNACH GOSPEL LECTIONARY. *Echternach. Middle of the eleventh century.*
*182 folios ($7^7/_8 \times 5^1/_2$"); many gold initials on colored ground, a few full-page; 6 small miniatures; 35 large miniatures.*
*Ms. 9428, f. 23*

ALTHOUGH ONE tends to use indiscriminately the words "Gospels" and "Gospel lectionary," these two terms should remain distinct. The Gospels are the four books of the New Testament which come in the following order: Matthew, Mark, Luke, and John. The Gospel lectionary is a liturgical book containing the passages of the Gospels which are read at Mass. This second category of manuscripts can be divided into two groups. In the older type, the Four Gospels follow each other, but they can be used for reading at Mass because of a kind of table which indicates the passages to be read at the feasts throughout the year. The Xanten Lectionary (plate 1) belongs to this group as well as the St. Lawrence Lectionary (plate 5). Later, it was realized that it would be much easier to copy those passages from the Gospels used at Mass one after the other, according to their usage during the liturgical year. Because of this parceling-out of the four inspired texts, these lectionaries were called pericopes. The dependence of this new category of books on the true Gospels appears in the double iconography of the Lectionary we are studying now. This illustration, indeed, starts with the representation of Christ and the four evangelists which is normal in the Gospels, either in a single miniature as in the Xanten manuscript (plate 1) or on several pages as in the St. Lawrence Lectionary (plate 5). In the Echternach Lectionary we have not only five full-page miniatures for this part of the decoration but also a series of miniatures that more specifically illustrate the pericopes.

The Healing of the Leper represented here decorates a page from Matthew's Gospel which is read on the third Sunday after the Epiphany. That such a large miniature should illustrate a rather unimportant day of this cycle shows that the illuminator did not decorate his manuscript in accordance with the liturgical importance of the feast; rather, he selected in the Gospels those passages which could be told in pictures because of their anecdotic quality. The extract from Matthew relates two miracles performed by Christ. Both are illustrated by a full-page miniature; curiously enough, on the previous Sunday, when John's account of the marriage at Cana is read, there is only one half-page miniature. The illuminator of this Lectionary was probably not directly responsible for the selection of the illustrations. Since this manuscript is one of the last made during the zenith of the Echternach school, it was certainly painted after iconographic programs in use for some time, and realized through the collaboration of several artists.

Matthew writes that one day, as Jesus was walking down from the mountain, followed by a great crowd, there came a leper to Him, beseeching Him and kneeling down to Him and saying to Him: "Lord, if thou wilt, thou canst make me clean." And Jesus, moved with compassion, put forth His hand and touched him and said to him: "I will; be thou clean." The illuminator has chosen the very moment when Christ is about to touch the leper. He is so literally faithful to the sacred text that he portrays Christ and His disciples in the act of descending the steep mountain slope. Needless to say, it was very bold on the part of a medieval artist to attempt such a difficult composition. The first following Jesus is probably St. Peter; he is visibly astonished to see Jesus touching the leper.

The soft and varied coloring found in the Lectionary is typical of several very luxurious manuscripts executed in the Abbey of Echternach. Under the Emperor's patronage the Benedictine monastery was encouraged to preserve and even to improve what may perhaps be considered the most beautiful style of illumination since Carolingian times. In the page presented here, the human cascade descending the side of the mountain, so novel in its iconographic plan, is further enhanced by the refined tones chosen by the painter. He owes this most beautiful of his creations to his strict observance of the text. His originality is even better displayed in his extraordinary use of a rich palette in decorating the grounds of his pictures. Above the diagonal line along which his characters are set, he has painted the background in horizontal colored strips of different widths and of either plain or shaded tints. In some places, in order to blend two contiguous contrasted colors, he has covered one with a broad layer of the other, as, for instance, in the upper edge of the blue surface which is painted over with a faint beige film. His original rendering of the mountainside is another example of the artist's exceptional gift for color. The whole Echternach atelier worked in this manner during the eleventh century and there will be a span of 300 years before medieval illuminators again find so rich a palette.

Another characteristic detail in this page is its very simple and classical frame, painted to suggest perspective by means of a graduated band of green and a thin white line which marks each angle. The study of frames would prove very useful to historians of the medieval miniature, for it would surely unearth some specific techniques of the various workshops. Is the very elaborate frame of our miniature inspired by frescoes, or is it the perfect result of its place in the evolution of the medieval book? This is one of the many unsolved problems, and we will come across it again in the following miniatures.

The story of this Lectionary is fairly well known. Certain data that it contains make it possible to date it around 1050. First, we find that great importance is given to St. Stephen in the text and the decoration of the Lectionary, which attest that this book was destined for a church or monastery of which this saint was the patron. Secondly, a thirteenth-century addition at the beginning of the codex includes the wording of the oath sworn by the Archbishop of Bremen at his election. As it happens, an archbishop of this town founded three priories around 1050, one of which was dedicated to St. Stephen. From other sources we know that Emperor Henry VII and his mother Gisela had formerly given the Archbishop of Bremen a token of their patronage, presenting him with a manuscript they had personally ordered in Echternach and which is now preserved in the State Library of Bremen. It is quite plausible that another manuscript should have been ordered in the same center, with a view to presenting it to the new monastery. The extraordinary qualities of the illuminated books made in Echternach and also the artistic and spiritual influence of this monastery were highly esteemed during the monastery's productive era.

## 5 The Evangelist Luke

ST. LAWRENCE GOSPEL LECTIONARY IN LIÈGE. *Probably Liège. Middle of the eleventh century.*
*182 folios ($13^3/_4 \times 10^1/_4$"); 5 large, several small initials; canon tables; 1 ornamental page; 2 unpainted sketches; 4 full-page miniatures.*
*Ms. 18383, f. 84 v*

THIS PAGE, with the three others in the St. Lawrence Gospel Lectionary, is generally considered to be a genuine product from the Meuse district of the German Empire. Critics even tend to be more explicit and ascribe the execution of this manuscript to the Benedictine Abbey of St. Lawrence in Liège, but there are no documents to back this opinion and the fact that this book is practically a unique specimen of its kind does not affirm this hypothesis more than any other. The problem is probably less clear-cut than is generally acknowledged. In any case this manuscript, because of its exceptional decoration, deserves to be considered one of the masterpieces of Romanesque miniature painting. The manuscript contains the Four Gospels, differing in this respect from the Echternach Lectionary (plate 4). But it is unquestionably a lectionary, for we find at the end a Comes, a table giving the passages to be read at each feast of the liturgical year. In this list the name of St. Lawrence is the only one to be underlined with red ink, showing that this book was destined for a monastery dedicated to him.

The division of the manuscript into four parts conditions its whole decoration. At the beginning of each Gospel we have a full-page miniature representing its author. Each portrait is followed by another page decorated completely with letters painted in large format: the *incipit* of the

LVCAS
EVGLA

corresponding Gospel. We have just seen a particularly rich example of these letters in the folio from the Wolbodon Psalter (plate 3). In addition, this Lectionary is ornamented by a decorative page (carpet design), very seldom encountered in manuscripts from the Meuse district. These full-page patterns come from insular books where they were used abundantly; they consisted of a framed page that was filled only with geometrical designs and schematic animals. The same decorative conception, evidently inspired by the insular style transmitted through Echternach, is applied here, although no use is made of the favorite Northumbrian ornaments.

The Evangelist Luke is facing us, seated on an X-shaped stool of which we see only two lions' heads and two paws, armed with claws, in the foreground. Near him is a writing lectern supporting a book. In his left hand is a horn used to contain ink; in the right he should normally hold a pen, but the illuminator seems to have forgotten this detail or perhaps did not notice it in his model. Directly or indirectly, the author of this painting depends on a Carolingian or even a Byzantine exemplar. He has taken up, rather casually, the components of his model without paying much attention to its subject or to its drawing; the decorative effect of the whole was what mainly concerned him. The artist obviously tried to paint the carpet on which the sacred author's feet appear in perspective, but he did not trouble to put in the lions' heads and the back legs of the seat that should normally appear on the back of it in the picture. We also notice that painting the lectern was a problem for him: its base is quite flat, whereas the lectern itself shows a serious effort in perspective. The classical model that inspired the artist is even more apparent in the knees and feet of the evangelist: left to his own devices he would never have chosen such an elaborate attitude. Since the legs extend in two opposite directions, there are two different positions for the feet. To draw this correctly some sense of space and volume on the part of the artist is needed. The rendering of the depth existed in the model, but the medieval artist contented himself with copying the drawing and could not express its spirit.

In spite of his shortcomings, the author of this miniature is a remarkable decorator. The draperies that clothe the sacred author are delightfully sophisticated; their folds display sheer fantasy, as if the painter were just seeking an opportunity to practice his talent. The background of the miniature is painted in two tints: a large surface of light purple bordered with white, a system we shall meet again later (plates 6 & 8). The frame is also carefully made: all the decorated pages of the manuscript are, like this one, surrounded with a band resembling a molding, painted between a gold and silver lintel. This border is more elaborate than the Echternach frame (plate 4), but it is also painted in perspective. Why should this type of border be used until the twelfth century, to be then ignored entirely during the Gothic period, at least until the end of the fourteenth century? It was probably not intended originally for the miniatures, but was inspired by objects of decoration that required such a border, as, for instance, ivory or enamel plates, and perhaps frescoes.

The St. Lawrence Lectionary is an archaeological document of primary importance for the study of the Romanesque art of illumination. First of all, it enables us to state without doubt that this remarkable work, started by one artist, was completed by another. The second miniaturist even dared to abandon the composition provided by his predecessor, and introduced into the Lectionary two extra folios illuminated by his own hand. He did not even take the trouble to rub out the two lead-pencil sketches already traced. Such independence is surprising, for in other respects this miniaturist conformed to the ideas of the first artist. The alternation of the evangelists, represented twice full-face and twice in profile, painted on a purple or gold background, is faithfully followed by the second master. The reason for this submissiveness may simply be due to the esteem, somewhat difficult for us to understand, in which this iconographic tradition was held by the medieval artisans. A comprehensive inquiry on the subject could provide valuable information. A close study of the first two miniatures in this manuscript reveals that they have been slightly retouched or finished by the second illuminator. We may therefore assume that the first artist died while still in the process of painting the first two miniatures, but after he had done the sketches of all four. His successor, who appears to have been at once so independent and so submissive, painted the two pages ascribed to his hand in the same style, with only a slightly different craftsmanship and more refinement. Hence we presume that some sort of atelier existed where a technical and iconographical tradition was preserved and transmitted. For a long time the general belief was that during the Romanesque period the monasteries executed their own miniature work. Now we think that, in most cases, the best works were made by traveling artists who settled where their talent was most required: near monasteries or bishoprics. If an atelier is in question, it is more understandable that it should become established in the neighborhood of a bishopric, since ornamented books were normally in greater demand there than in monasteries. It seems therefore quite natural to assign the artists who have illuminated our Lectionary to Liège rather than any other center. This localization is further confirmed by the difference in style between this book and manuscripts belonging to another group from the Meuse district that we shall soon see (plate 8).

The St. Lawrence Lectionary evidently dates back to the eleventh century. Unfortunately we do not know yet what important event would account for the preparation of such a luxurious book.

# 6 St. Gregory the Great and His Deacon Peter

ST. GREGORY THE GREAT. Dialogues. *Meuse, perhaps Liège. End of the twelfth century.*
*152 folios ($10^{7}/_{8} \times 7^{3}/_{4}$"); numerous initials in three colors; 60 initials; full-page frontispiece.*
*Ms. 9916–17, f. 1 v*

THE FULL-PAGE MINIATURE reproduced here has the two-fold merit of being a superb example of a frontispiece miniature representing a medieval author, and one of the most beautiful specimens of illumination from the Meuse district. By comparing it with the page added to the Xanten Gospels (plate 1) which represents a profane author, we have a better insight into the contrast between the execution in these two epochs, even if the purple parchment folio is a Carolingian copy of an antique picture. Indeed, we can see at first glance how deeply this frontispiece folio of the *Dialogues* is impregnated with religious spirit. St. Gregory, the pope, wearing a miter, is sitting on a special kind of stool: it is the top of a fluted column with a cushion placed on its capital. He holds in his left hand a copy of the *Dialogues*, while his right reaches toward a dove which is whispering in his ear: an expressive way of conveying celestial inspiration. Here, however, is a detail needing some explanation: the dove has one foot on the saint's shoulder while the other rests on what might resemble a perch, except that it has at one end a golden decorative ornament that may also be seen on the saint's other shoulder. A closer look reveals that these ornaments are two golden knots at the end of the ribbons that hang from behind the miter. The weakness of the drawing is responsible for the apparent stiffness of this ornament; on the left shoulder it is bent and follows the curves of the mantle.

Facing the author is a scribe seated on a socle, similar to the one that we shall see in the Mosan Gospel (plate 8). We know from the saint's life that he was helped in his work by the deacon Peter. We hardly need draw attention to the religious garments of the copyist, nor to his size, which is a good deal smaller than that of the pope. By adopting a different scale for his subjects the miniaturist has simply conformed to the traditional iconography which required that God and those consecrated to His service should be endowed with a larger stature than ordinary mortals. The scribe holds two tablets which, for no apparent reason, are painted in two different colors. There is no doubt that these are tablets, for one can see in the deacon's other hand a sharp stylet that will be used to mark the wax, instead of the pen that is held by most medieval copyists (plates 8 & 32). The scribe thrusts this stylet through the drapery that hangs in the center of the picture between Gregory and himself without, however, preventing them from seeing each other. Such a gesture is simply impossible to account for in this picture. To find out what is meant, one must refer to an earlier iconography. There, indeed, may be found a theme in which the copyist likewise pierces with his stylet the hangings that completely separate him from the author. The reason for this gesture is to enable the scribe to see through the little hole at his master, who is dictating under the burning flow of inspiration. Representing the curtains tied up together was not a very bright idea on our miniaturist's part, for he has sacrificed a lifelike iconography for the sake of a somewhat baroque fancy, typical of the late Romanesque period.

The background of this scene, which is indeed beautiful in spite of its weaknesses, is plain blue, framed with green. This is a typical decorative style for the backgrounds of miniatures in manuscripts executed in the Meuse area during the twelfth century. We shall encounter it again in a lectionary (plate 8) which is scarcely later than these *Dialogues* of St. Gregory. Here the green frame is shaped like the architectural arcade that encloses the whole scene. This important decoration comprises two features: first the main columns and the arch joining them, then the architectural motifs that surmount them. The columns, together with their Roman socle and capital, are derived from Roman arches of a form that was used even before the Carolingian period to enframe the canons, that is to say, the concordance tables of the Gospels. The upper part with its bell turrets, its cupola tower, and its walls has, on the contrary, an architectural background of Byzantine origin; one can see a similar type of architecture in a Cologne miniature painted about the same time (plate 7). We may also trace the evolution of the Roman arch, of the sort used in Merovingian manuscripts, in some frames of the Gothic miniatures of the mid-fourteenth century, for instance, in a missal presumably made in Brussels (plate 13). The wall at the top of the picture is painted with an extreme accuracy that deserves to be noticed, but, while the building is perfectly symmetrical and should have been painted in a parallel perspective, the little windowpanes are drawn and painted as if they were seen from the right. The miniaturist copied those frames on each side of the central tower but without depth, because he did not understand his model.

In these *Dialogues*, St. Gregory tells the story of several saints worshiped especially in Italy, giving a choice place to St. Benedict. The sixty miniatures decorating our copy constitute a true illustration of these texts. This is the continuation of a classic tradition that we have already seen employed, in a very informal style, in the *Psychomachia* (plate 2) and even in the Echternach Gospel Lectionary (plate 4). During the Romanesque period, miniatures seldom have such an anecdotic character: they are usually confined to decorative purposes. This copy of the *Dialogues* is therefore exceptional and announces the Gothic age which will delight in pictorial representations and will, besides, express them in other techniques, such as stained glass and tapestry. The grandeur of this frontispiece folio, laying emphasis on the author and on his assistant, is also the sign of a new era. It should be borne in mind, however, that the author is an ecclesiastic and that his work is eminently religious; in the Romanesque period a manuscript of such importance and quality is unthinkable in connection with a secular text.

The pictorial technique of this page is less linear, less obviously metallic, than that of the Meuse Gospel we shall see further on (plate 8), and is less closely related to enamel craft. The features are softer, the folds more supple or, rather, less angular. Some of the illuminations could even be considered true paintings, for the artist relies much more on his skillful use of coloring than on his drawing. This cannot be said unreservedly, though, for the artist who shared with the principal master the work of illustrating occasionally displays such a schematic style that he draws what look like ellipse-shaped thigh-guards, instead of folds, to cover legs.

This manuscript, undoubtedly from the Meuse area, which was in the possession of the St. Lawrence Abbey in Liège as far back as the thirteenth century, seems to have been destined for the Collegiate Church of St. John. Indeed, the last miniature displays the offering of the book by its scribe, who humbly bends his knee to the Apostle John while presenting him his copy of the *Dialogues*. Until further investigation of the remarkable production of the Meuse valley, the end of the twelfth century is generally agreed upon as the date of execution of this Lectionary.

7

# Christ Washing the Feet of the Apostles

EVANGELIARY FOR THE USE OF THE BENEDICTINE ABBEY OF SS. MARTIN AND ELIPH IN COLOGNE. *School of Cologne. About 1200.*
*193 folios ($9^3/_4 \times 8^1/_2$"); 29 full-page miniatures; several initials.*
*Ms. 9222, f. 87 v*

THE PAINTING represented here lies opposite the Gospel of Holy Thursday and shows the event as it was described by John, whose Gospel is read on this day.

The scheme of the picture is unusually bold: Christ has been painted outside the frame; the illuminator has then arranged the twelve Apostles so that they converge towards Him, grouping them in such a harmonious way that the general result is a feeling of perfect balance. Moreover, the realism he has here contrived to attain is seldom found in the beginning of the thirteenth century; even the fourteenth century remains generally ignorant of such spontaneity as appears, for instance, in the attitudes of Jesus and Peter. In this respect Peter's gestures are particularly striking; his acute embarrassment is eloquently expressed by the position of his arms and hands.

Such progress in the representation of the human figure is in strong contrast with the archaism still prevailing in the background of the miniature, with its large surfaces covered with burnished gold and its sketchy architectural elements. The Romanesque spirit still maintained its grip in a milieu that was, however, one of the first to acknowledge new aesthetic values. The coloring still partially conforms with the tradition of the twelfth century, particularly in the use of the reds and greens which are practically the only colors to be found in the

164

ornamental architecture and in the framework of the miniature. The very concept of this frame, made of parallel lines painted in a variety of colors, is a survival of the Romanesque manner, because it is not concerned with perspective. One cannot deny, however, that the miniature proper shows a real effort to enrich the traditional palette.

The technique of painting is also noticeably more original. First, the artist has overlaid the dark strokes of his drawing with flat colors that vary according to the different parts of the clothing; then, by painting over this first coat with different shades, he has brought forth the effects of light and shadow. Elsewhere he has done just the opposite, again tracing firm dark strokes over the first layer so as to emphasize the movements of the folds. Along with these two processes so diametrically opposed to each other, we may observe that the illuminator nevertheless proclaims the approach of Gothic art by his sensitiveness to the folds of the clothing, while still belonging to the Romanesque period in his manner of drawing the human body. By keeping the two tendencies in balance he asserts himself as a link between two ages.

A perfect example of this new spirit is to be found in another miniature in this same Gospel Lectionary. This is evident in its coloring in which blue predominates, in its frame, decorated with greater variety, and in its motifs which introduce such novelties as Greek fretwork. This miniature, strangely enough, belongs to the first page of the first quire. One is tempted to ascribe it to some master illuminator who, though more progressive than his contemporaries, was still working with a team of collaborators painting in the traditional style. The first quire of the Lectionary is written in an entirely different hand from the rest of the text: a Gothic script, unquestionably clearer and newer. The first miniature in this quire is contemporary with the entire book. But the first quire, either because it was damaged or worn out, may have had to be replaced. Since the Gospel Lectionary was most probably entrusted to the workshop of its origin when in need of repair, two important periods in the production of one and the same center may thus be preserved for us. In such cases as this, only the archaeological examination of the codex can help us to decide whether the difference in the style is due to rehandling, or to the collaboration of contemporary craftsmen with different cultural backgrounds and with their own particular processes.

From the contents of the manuscript proper, we may assume that the writing was done by monks, the very monks perhaps for whose abbey the Lectionary was intended. But the miniatures show the same technique as that of contemporary mural-painting and they have also a similar style. The miniatures are therefore probably the work of laymen.

The illustration of the Gospels is divided into three parts: the Christmas cycle, the Easter cycle, and a few special feast days. Some particular features of the iconography and a few oddities in the order of the miniatures need to be outlined. In addition to the Nativity and the Adoration of the Magi, the Christmas cycle includes the Dream of St. Joseph and the Tree of Jesse, which are seldom encountered in the series. The feast of the Circumcision has no illustration but there is an additional picture for the first Sunday of Advent: it is a miniature representing the Entry into Jerusalem. This subject in this place can only be understood as symbolic of the coming of Christ to earth. The Easter cycle is longer and begins with the Temptation of Christ and the Miracle of the Loaves and Fishes. Then come the main events relating to the Passion, the Resurrection, the Ascension, and the Descent of the Holy Ghost. However, the miniatures do not always appear in the same order as the events they describe; for instance, the Washing of the Feet of the Apostles comes after the Crucifixion and the Descent from the Cross. This discrepancy is due to the fact that the latter two decorate two narrations of the Passion which are read during Holy Week, whereas the Washing of the Feet of the Apostles is the illustration for Maundy Thursday. The Last Supper, which should normally come after the Washing of the Feet of the Apostles, is in the beginning of the manuscript: it is this miniature, of a more evolved style belonging to an additional and partly remade quire, which was just discussed above. This anomaly could be the result either of some development in the paschal liturgy, or of a mistake in the execution of the Lectionary. In any case the text accompanying this painting concerns the Easter cycle since it begins with the following words: *Ante diem festum Pasche.*

The third series of miniatures represents a few feast days of Christ and of the Virgin, as well as certain saint's days celebrated by the whole Church, those of St. John the Baptist, SS. Peter and Paul, and St. Mary Magdalen. The Meeting of Jesus with Zacchaeus decorates the feast of the consecration of the church.

The manuscript was meant for the use of the Benedictine Abbey of St. Martin and St. Eliph, as is evident from the list of saints who were the object of special worship. Each one of the numerous miniatures illustrates some important feast in the Church calendar, and there is only one saint to have the Gospel of his feast adorned with a miniature: St. Martin, patron of the abbey.

Until further evidence is produced, we may presume that the decoration of the Evangeliary was entrusted to one of the local ateliers in Cologne. The traditions flourishing there were certainly rich enough to explain the exceptional quality of this manuscript. A fuller knowledge of the history of the monastery might bring to light the event, certainly an important one, for which this superb manuscript was made.

## 8 The Nativity; The Evangelist Matthew

MOSAN GOSPEL LECTIONARY. *Valley of the Meuse River. End of the thirteenth century.*
*60 folios ($5^1/_4 \times 3''$); 3 large and many small initials; 5 miniatures, 4 of them full-page.*
*Ms. 10527, ff. 15 v and 16 r*

IN THE HISTORY of illumination in the Meuse valley, contacts had evidently been established between the techniques of the contemporary production of enamels and the traditional patterns and iconographies of Romanesque illumination. To both crafts this contact brought an enrichment that has not been sufficiently studied. The double page reproduced here dates from this period of exchange and interpenetration. It shows the Nativity, placed at the beginning of St. Matthew's Gospel, and a portrait of the evangelist himself.

The Virgin is reclining on a couch, propped up by a cushion and leaning on her right elbow. Her head rests on her right hand in which she clutches a kind of coif worn over her head. The other arm lies gracefully on the bedclothes that cover her. This very natural position and the simple gesture of the right hand are rather surprising in a picture of such a schematic character. The upper end of the bed is supported by two legs, but there seem to be none at the other end. Their absence is perhaps intentional; the reason will be better understood later. Joseph is seated on a type of socle, the gesture of his arm and hand expressing his wonder at the birth which has just taken place. The parchment scroll in his left hand suggests that the Child's earthly father had been reading the prophecies announcing the coming of the Messiah. The Child Jesus, with the usual cruciform halo, is lying in a carefully decorated manger placed on the ground. The hillocks below the crib signify the earth and are a conventional representation

LIBER
I

dating back to the ninth century; we have already encountered another example in the Prudentius manuscript (plate 2).

The curious distribution of the characters in this Nativity would certainly puzzle us were it not explained by a similar iconography in an earlier manuscript. There was, indeed, a kind of "two-storied" Nativity in art after the eleventh century. There is one in the Echternach Gospels (plate 4) and another in the Averbode Gospels in the Liège University Library; the latter may be considered the direct ancestor of this Mosan manuscript. In both these books the picture is divided into two completely different sections, showing the Virgin and Joseph in the lower part and the Child, the donkey, and the ox in the upper. That our miniature derives from the Nativity of Liège will soon become evident from the many features that the two pictures have in common. In both Mary is reclining and holding her veil with one hand; Jesus is lying close to the heads of the animals, and Joseph is seated on the same kind of socle. But in the Brussels miniature the composition has undergone a complete change. It is no longer, strictly speaking, a two-storied Nativity, since all the characters are gathered in the same place; however, since the manger, or crib, is placed so high, it must be the Liège miniature which served as the model for this artist.

This change in the distribution of the characters had other consequences: in order to attain one realistic aspect the painter sacrifices others. This time the subject could not be painted the width of the model. The Virgin's bed had to be inclined to avoid reducing the size of the characters and also to fill the page. This is why the legs at the foot of the bed, clearly visible in the Averbode miniature, are entirely missing here. Again the restriction in width obliges Joseph, who in the model is standing on the same level as the Virgin, to be moved further up. Instead of a symmetrical composition we have here a much more daring page, where the figures are distributed in such a way as to avoid empty spaces. Even in condensing his subject, the illuminator remained obedient to this *horror vacui* imposed on medieval artists.

Is it too bold to say that these Gospels are already much more Gothic than Romanesque? The iconography of the Averbode manuscript is, indeed, more conventional, more classical, and also more theological, for the two-storied Nativity is the result of a religious conception opposed to the representation of God and human beings on the same level, even where the Virgin was concerned. Our Gospel being smaller, the subject is in a way humanized; it is only the starting point of a long evolution. Let us call to mind the fifteenth-century Nativities, still saturated with fervor, that are realistic to the point of showing the Child lying on a bed of straw.

The birth of Christ is the subject chosen by the illuminator to decorate the Gospel of Matthew. Each of the Gospels is preceded with a scene from the life of Christ: the Death on the Cross for Mark, the Holy Women by the Tomb for Luke, and the Ascension for John. The Nativity is a very appropriate choice for Matthew, whose Gospel starts with a long genealogy of Christ. In the miniature on the right-hand page, the evangelist has written on the manuscript laid open in front of him: *Liber gene* for *Liber generationis Jesu Christi*, which are the first words of the text. The word *Liber* appears again on a large strip beside the miniature, and beneath follows the rest of the text. The evangelist is seated on a socle identical with that of Joseph in the opposite picture; the folds of his mantle are more archaic than those seen in the full-page miniature. The strongly marked outline of his leg reminds one of a thigh-guard and is definitely Romanesque, whereas the folds of the Virgin's mantle and bedcover hardly reveal the line of the body and become decorative in themselves. Thus, we notice once again a trend toward more realism after a period of stylization. As in most medieval representations of an author, Matthew is seen holding a pen, and a knife which was used to scratch out mistakes and to sharpen the calamus.

Apart from these stylistic aspects attesting that the manuscript was executed during a period of transition, some technical particularities also deserve to be mentioned. The dominant colors are red and blue; all traces of the green that was still found in the *Dialogues* of St. Gregory the Great (plate 6) and in the Cologne Gospel Lectionary (plate 7) have here entirely disappeared. These colors are used as a frame, the red surrounding the blue, to enclose the background of the miniature in a more rigorous and geometrical manner than was previously the custom. From the pictorial point of view, the artist has outlined the details of his miniature with excessive vigor, but this is understandable if one compares it with enamel work. Enamel, especially cloisonné, has neatly delineated color areas comparable to those of stained glass. The volute on the evangelist's right shoulder shows very clearly the influence of this metal craft. An almost identical motif on Joseph's leg retains the same character to some extent, but it has in addition evolved into a more pictorial decoration. One should not conclude too hastily that this miniature was the work of enamelers, or that the artist could practice indifferently one craft or the other. The question remains open to discussion. We may take for certain, on the other hand, that the same cartoons were used by both.

That our Gospels are as closely related to the Averbode Gospels (Liège, University Library, Ms. 363 b), or even to the Floreffe Bible (British Museum, Ms. Additional 17.737–17.738), as it is to enamels executed in the Meuse valley, is irrefutable. This remarkable, though comparatively small, manuscript may be ascribed to the Meuse valley, but it would be presumptuous to suggest a more precise location. It seems later than either of the above-named works, certainly more recent than the Averbode Gospels. It is already more Gothic in spirit, which tends to indicate that this Brussels manuscript is the last of that group, dating from a period that is not so distant from 1200 as is generally thought.

# 9 Doubting Thomas

PSALTER OF GUY DE DAMPIERRE. *Northern France. About 1270.*
*245 folios ($4^1/_4 \times 3''$); 12 illustrations for the calendar; 10 full-page miniatures; 8 initials; many grotesques.*
*Ms. 10607, ff. 149 v and 150 r*

THIS FULL-PAGE MINIATURE represents the encounter of Christ with his disciple in a rather unrealistic and oversimplified manner, in order to preserve a somewhat monumental style in spite of the diminutive size of the manuscript. The scene shows only these two principal characters, although Thomas is supposed to have confessed his faith in the presence of the other Apostles. Also, the tree in the background indicates an outdoor scene, which is not in accordance with Gospel texts. The architectural design at the top of the miniature, though it shows some new features, continues in the Byzantine and Romanesque tradition that we see so faithfully preserved in the Cologne Gospel Lectionary (plate 7).

The miniature is set in an intricate frame, the coloring and decoration of which are definitely Gothic. Its angles have been enlarged to include medallions with coats of arms which, judging by the many armorial shields in the manuscript, belong to important Flemish families (La Motte? Moerseke?). By allowing his subject to overlap the frame the illuminator reveals how unconventional he could be. In this case the feet of the two figures, as well as Christ's fingers holding the victorious banner of the Resurrection, are painted outside the frame. Since there are only a few of the last verses of Psalm 94 written at the top of folio 150, one can see that the text is interrupted by the miniature. This picture is, therefore, an additional decoration to

the illuminated initial *C* at the beginning of Psalm 95: *Cantate Dominum canticum novum.* Folio 150 shows three singers standing before a lectern.

We must not allow the splendor of these two miniatures to blind us to the beauty of the marginal decoration, which is a masterpiece. Its symbolism is pleasantly whimsical and shows at times an excellent sense of humor. Is there a touch of anticlericalism in the armored figure whose sword is tickling the nose of a terrified and grimacing monk? There is no doubt about the rabbit who blows a horn, while a dog is on the point of eating its quarry, the hunter it has just caught! So as to make quite clear his intention of representing a topsy-turvy world, the illuminator completes the picture by showing us the rabbit coming home from the hunt with its spoils thrown over its shoulder.

The text and its ornamental details are not lacking in merit. The Gothic handwriting is well-formed, free of stiffness. The line endings are slightly out of proportion. The rich colors and gold that illuminate the initial are poured lavishly into the margin. The whole setting of the page displays a wonderful sense of the art of bookmaking, both spontaneous and well-balanced.

The manuscript is decorated throughout in the same lively style. The calendar is adorned on each page with a scene depicting work typical of that month of the year. The subjects are painted broadly but with the same refinement that we admire in the great miniatures. This background of burnished gold was cherished by the master illuminators of the thirteenth century and was still in favor with the Dutch right up to the middle of the fifteenth century. The Psalter itself opens with a full-page letter *B* standing for *Beatus*. According to tradition, this *B* was always lavishly ornamented, sometimes with other letters of the word, sometimes even with several of the following words (plate 3). Here the rest of the *Beatus* has been omitted, the next folio continuing with *Vir qui non abiit*. . . . The scribe was therefore expecting the illuminator to include the full word in his page.

The hundred and fifty psalms are divided into eight groups. The first begins with the large letter *B* as described above and the others with a decorated initial of a smaller size, the subject of which bears no relation to the text. These initials form the basic decoration of the psalms. Probably because it was made for such an important dignitary, this codex contains ten more full-page miniatures which, except for one, were inserted into the original quires. The first ones recall the childhood of Christ, and the last his Passion. The *B* of *Beatus*, together with the two miniatures painted in its lobes, happens to supply the link between these two iconographic cycles: the miniature in the top shows the Flight into Egypt, the lower one the Entry into Jerusalem. This contrast was certainly intended by the illuminator.

The miniatures are remarkably drawn, at once supple and firm. The coloring is simple but pleasant. Blues and ochers, so characteristic of early Gothic miniatures, are here predominant.

The backgrounds are uniformly of burnished gold, their fresh brilliance showing the degree of perfection attained in the technique of applying gold leaf. A number of the saints worshiped in northern France are mentioned in the calendar and litanies. The names of Winnoc, Omer, Bertin, and Folquin indicate more precisely the bishopric of Thérouanne. It is in any case to this part of France that we should turn our thoughts when ascribing an origin for not only this Psalter, but for many others of a similar style.

The patron for whom the manuscript was made is well known: Guy de Dampierre, count of Flanders. This we can tell from his coat of arms which often appears in the Psalter. The escutcheons of several of his many children enable us to ascertain that the manuscript was made after 1266, the birthdate of his son, Jean de Namur, and before the death of another son, Baudouin, in 1275. The count had also many other coats of arms painted in his codex, probably to remind him of important dignitaries of his court.

In the history of the medieval book, this manuscript for Guy de Dampierre may be considered one of the most successful examples of a particular sort of work: the psalter of small format, intended for laymen, its miniatures glittering with gold and displaying a wealth of fantasy on every page. The new spirit from which springs Gothic art was a spirit of rebellion from the very beginning and its mark is clear in this group of manuscripts. In the Romanesque period, books and the arts pertaining to books were almost exclusively concerned with God, and with the people consecrated to Him or entrusted with His authority. The result was an incredible number of liturgical and hagiographic texts. With the coming of the Gothic age, not only does man rebel against the powers that had restrained him before, but he deliberately chooses a language of his own, which he prefers to Latin, to express human values that had not previously been treated. Even in pious texts and prayer books such as this Psalter, when made in newly formed communes, there is a breath of liberty, enthusiastic and confident.

This irresistible impulse, which had already manifested itself at the end of the twelfth century, seems to have first been used to express motion and life. In the history of Gothic illumination, northwestern France was perhaps, with northern Italy, one of the creative centers in which this new force found its most successful expression. Fifteenth-century humanism would not have been possible without this revolution.

10

# Psalter Page in Gold and Blue Letters

THE PETERBOROUGH PSALTER. *East Anglia. Probably 1299.*
*161 folios ($11^3/_4 \times 7^3/_4$"); double illustrations for the calendar; 31 pages decorated with four pictures each; 3 miniatures with nonreligious subjects; 11 historiated initials; margins and countless line endings with grotesques.*
*Ms. 9961–62, f. 74*

THIS PSALTER is so lavishly illustrated that it is difficult to decide which is the most beautiful page. From the point of view of originality, preference may well be given to the pages written in letters of gold. In these pages the initials have been treated with as much care as the miniatures, and the pages are remarkable besides for their matchless display of marginal decoration. Folio 74 was given a particular decoration because it coincides with a division of the Psalter beginning with Psalm 109: *Dixit Dominus Domino meo. . . .* The initial, an uncial *D*, includes a scene illustrating the text. The picture shows Christ sitting at the Father's right hand, the dove of the Holy Ghost between them. This initial extends around the text on all sides of the page. Hanging from the baguette at the top are the coats of arms of the duchies of Flanders and Limburg, added to the manuscript in the fifteenth century. The other extension from the *D* hangs downward along the left margin to include ornament, grotesques, and birds. It continues across the bottom of the page, where it becomes the stand of a scene inspired by chivalry. A knight, who has just dismounted from his horse, is lying on the grass in his coat of mail. He holds a mirror for a young damsel who is busy braiding her hair in the shade of a blossoming shrub. A little to one side stands a maidservant holding a large stone; she is threatening an intruder who seeks to disturb the young couple by throwing pebbles. The baguette continues up the

outside right margin with a column of angel musicians. Each angel plays a different instrument and the mandorla encircling him rests very gracefully on the wings of the musician beneath. At the top of the page a maiden kneels in the attitude of a donor; she wears a very fine veil which falls to her shoulders and a crown upon her head. We may find in the manuscript elements that would help to identify this young person. To complete the description of the page we should not fail to point out the extraordinary variety of the line endings; they show the inexhaustible imagination of the craftsmen in the field of decoration.

In spite of its richness this one folio cannot give us a complete idea of the magnificence of the whole Psalter. Opposite the pages written in gold letters there are folios written entirely in blue, and others, where one column of the text is written in blue and the other in gold. There is no other manuscript of the Gothic period to be found which is entirely written in these two colors and the general effect is wonderful. Similar refinements in the technique are to be seen in the preparation of the vellum itself before receiving the transcribed text. The alternation of the rulings applied here is one of the most elaborate to be found in the history of the medieval book; they alternate in color in opposition to the gold or blue letters that the scribe is expected to trace above them.

Like the manuscript of Guy de Dampierre (plate 9), the Peterborough Psalter is divided into eight sections which are distinct from each other since they all begin at the top of a page. Each section is preceded by a variable number of folios on which pictures have been painted, four to a page. These pictures correspond two by two; in each the illuminator represents an event of the Old Testament which prefigures an important fact in the New. There are about one hundred of these miniatures, forming an extensive compendium of iconography. The themes have been borrowed largely from the stained-glass windows of Canterbury and from the frescoes of the Abbey of Peterborough, for this masterpiece was destined for the abbot there.

From the pictorial aspect, these miniatures are certainly not inferior to those of the rest of the manuscript. If we are sometimes startled by green and orange coloring, we are charmed, on the other hand, by the variety of tints and the exquisite shading. Two miniaturists have worked on this Psalter and, from the point of view of color, one is more creative than his colleague. His paintings, though more crowded, are also more balanced. There still remains a certain awkwardness in the gestures but they are quite remarkable in the way they express action. The faces sometimes even display sentiments, especially those painted by the second artist.

The calendar states that the Psalter was made for the Benedictine Abbey of Peterborough, but its parts were not completed at one time. The Psalter itself absorbed almost all the productivity of the scribes and illuminators who worked on it. When we come to folio 94, the gold is less brilliant and less evenly applied, seemingly laid on in haste. From there on the rulings are all traced with black lead and the line endings reduced to mere geometrical patterns. This part includes a selection of prayers, probably personal, among which is one to St. Guthlac, patron saint of the neighboring Abbey of Croyland. In fact, we know from historical data that this Psalter was ordered for Godfrey of Croyland in view of his appointment to office in 1299. It seems as if the Psalter was written and decorated at leisure for the abbot-to-be of Peterborough before he was designated; but, when Godfrey was elected, the craftsmen had to hasten to add the favorite prayers of the new abbot. It is he whom we see painted on the front page of the Psalter, kneeling at the feet of Christ. Later on, when the manuscript passed into French hands, someone wrote "St. Benoît" on the large black mantle of the Benedictine monk. Further on in the codex there are two people represented in the attitude of donors: one of them is the damsel mentioned above and the other a knight-at-arms. Their presence here, their size, and the place they hold in the Psalter would be difficult to account for, unless they are relatives of the abbot, perhaps his brother and sister, and the donors of the manuscript.

This Psalter *en lettres d'or et d'azur* has an intricate history and we are fortunate to know at least these essential details. Owing to its characteristic blue and gold coloring, it is referred to with the above title in all the different inventories of the collections in which it was kept. Abbot Godfrey presented the precious manuscript to the Cardinal Gaucelin d'Euse when the latter visited Peterborough. The Cardinal, in turn, offered it to his uncle, Pope John XXII, from whom it passed to the library of Clemence of Hungary, wife of Louis X, king of France. When this collection was dispersed, it was bought by Philip IV of France, and became part of the library of the Louvre. From there it went to the library of the dukes of Burgundy, but not before the reign of Philip the Good for there is no mention of the Psalter *en lettres d'or et d'azur* in 1420 in the inventory of John the Fearless, father of Philip the Good. That is the reason why the coats of arms of the *Grand Duc d'Occident* and of his various states and possessions are frequently found in the margins of the Peterborough Psalter. It was probably taken from the Louvre because of its magnificence and the new owner, wanting to make sure of keeping it, put in many marks of his ownership.

## 11 The Nativity; The Annunciation to the Shepherds; The Adoration of the Magi

GALLUS, Chronologia Sacra. *Northern Spain. Beginning of the fourteenth century.*
*30 folios ($16^1/_8 \times 11''$); decoration on all pages; many medallions; 4 large pictures; a Crucifixion covering 2 pages.*
*Ms. 9174, f. 27*

THE BIRTH OF CHRIST holds an important place in the "Sacred Chronology"; it is therefore one of the most important miniatures of this abundantly illustrated manuscript.

The draftsman or the illuminator responsible for the arrangement of the extensive iconography at his disposal presents the different scenes of the Nativity in the same medallion design that is generally adopted in the whole manuscript. This setting endows the miniature with a somewhat monumental effect: one can easily imagine it transposed into the main rose window of a Gothic cathedral. The architectural aspect is further accentuated by the three-cusped arches encircling the medallion.

In the center of the picture three iconographic themes have been rather successfully blended. The scene of the Nativity in the middle combines traditions from varying sources. Mary, the Child, Joseph, and the animals are not grouped in the grotto or even in its entrance, but outside. The grotto is clearly represented, however, by a black area surrounded by brown rocks. The manger, shaped like a sarcophagus, occupies the center of the picture and is placed along the horizontal axis of the painting. But the whole scene is made slightly unsymmetrical by the reclining position of the Virgin which enables her to reach and cover the Child. The Annunciation to the Shepherds is shown on the right at the top of the picture, whereas the Adoration

Augustus. cesar
Tyberi. cesar

of the Magi is down on the left. A few sheep are painted into the foreground to fill the empty space.

Each of the sixteen Prophets gathered around this main scene is accompanied by the angel who inspired him. They are grouped so as to converge toward the center, while still respecting verticality. Jeremiah, for instance, who is located at the base of the medallion, does not turn his head toward the outer edge of the circle but toward the inner. Each Prophet points with his finger to the Child while holding a scroll that bears his prophesies about the coming of the Messiah in the other hand.

The medallion seems to rest upon three colored lines which go through the page; these reappear on every folio of the manuscript. They symbolize in this Chronology the direct and continuous descent of Christ from Abraham. The two small medallions at the right are completely independent, because the figures they represent – the Emperors Augustus and Tiberius – do not belong to the genealogy of Jesus.

The *Chronologia Sacra*, sometimes called *The Tree of Biblical History*, is conceived as a succession of portraits representing the best-known characters of the Bible. The more important ones have a commentary, sometimes covering half a page, reminding us of their role in history. This is the case, for instance, with Jacob, Daniel, and several others. The biblical genealogy covers the right-hand and left-hand pages of each folio and continues through thirty folios. It begins with pictures of Adam and Eve which occupy the top of the first two open pages and ends in the same way, on the last two, with an impressive Crucifixion. This last miniature is encircled by a frame showing the twenty-four Prophets who announced the sufferings and the death of Christ. The two extreme points of the *Chronologia Sacra* are linked by the three colored stripes already described; these stripes schematically represent a tree. Along this central line, medallions succeed each other, their sizes varying according to the importance of the people represented; Noah, Abraham, and, above all, David are especially honored. From the main stem spring a great number of branches arranged exactly as in genealogical trees of the present day; they bear small medallions decorated with the bust of the person whose name is mentioned. Certain other medallions stand alone because they bear no relation to the Chronology. A few subjects have been emphasized because they have special importance: Isaiah, who foretold the fall of Babylon; the Annunciation; the Nativity described above; and Jesus among the Doctors. The setting of the text as well as its decoration lead us to think that this manuscript is a transposition of a genealogical tree originally made on a continuous roll. The idea of the medallions, however, seems to have been inspired by the art of stained-glass windows.

The *Chronologia Sacra* is more impressive for the originality of its ornamental conception than for the quality of its miniatures. Its contents never fail to satisfy our curiosity and the book can certainly be considered exceptional, even when compared with the best of the various productions found in the history of illumination. In this accumulation of medallions and portraits the artisan has managed to avoid the stumbling block of repetition. Although the faces may have been somewhat summarily drawn, the composition is harmonious and the coloring attractive, with the exception of the rays of light which are rendered with strokes of white paint and the heavy black strokes depicting shadow. Apart from this shortcoming the illuminator seems to have possessed a good range of colors. He remains outstanding for his accurate portrayal of movement. The *Chronologia Sacra* dates back to the beginning of the fourteenth century and, because of the type of handwriting and the style of the miniatures, can probably be ascribed to Spain. It has not been possible so far to ascertain whether it comes from Aragon or from Castile.

12

# The Chamberlain of the King of Majorca

THE PALATINE LAWS OF JAMES II OF MAJORCA. *Majorca. 1337.*
*79 folios (15$^3/_4$ × 10"); 8 miniatures; 68 initials with ornaments; important marginal decoration with a few grotesques.*
*Ms. 9169, f. 52 v*

IN LUXURIOUS MANUSCRIPTS destined for princely patrons the miniatures were usually set neatly apart from the text. On this very elegant page the two are, somewhat unexpectedly, quite freely interwoven.

On the right we see the room containing the royal wardrobe. The garments are hanging on a long coat rail and a huge chest fills the rear of the chamber. In the foreground a man is busy working at a robe laid on the table; he is about to fold it up or perhaps add a last stitch. His colleague is vigorously shaking other clothing, presumably before refolding it. It seems they have just been receiving orders from one of the king's attendants who is accompanied by a servant; this attendant is probably the chamberlain responsible for the royal wardrobe.

This high official, armed with a sword, and his companion are represented inside the palace; they are standing in a large hall built in the form of a rotunda and surrounded by an arcade. The place where the clothing is kept must be one of the several rooms grouped around the central hall and, we suppose, opening onto its circular arcade. The hall is covered with a coffered cupola shown in remarkably good perspective; the flat ceiling of the porch is also effectively adorned with the same coffering. The whole architectural structure is enhanced by slender spires with parts of the text inserted between them. The general coloring is of different shades of green, popular with Italian illuminators.

nõ duaꝝ sellarum / habentium
coria nõ coopta veluto / anno
quolibet / una pxīm ante fes
tum bti iohis bap / sic hoc dicto
laudabili ordinamꝰ. Altera
autē pxīm ante festū bti mi
chaelis archangeli volumꝰ
adimpleri. Preterea octo
saltim sellas armoꝝ usui des
tinatas p nre psone fructio
habeamꝰ. quaꝝ due sint nro
signo Regio penitus decoratē
Reliq nō sint aliis opibꝰ nre
voluntati placentibꝰ exornatē.
Iubemus etiam qꝫ quatuor
saltī mante continue sit pate

ad regem dum dictas sellas nre
psone fructio destinatas qꝛ
due sint nri signi regii i su
is ptibꝰ munitis. alie autē
due sint diūsis opibꝰ cōmu
nite. Postremo subiungi
mꝰ plibatis qꝫ adsit cōtinue
copia mantaꝝ ac aliaꝝ reꝝ
necessariaꝝ / equis et ceteris
animalibꝰ antedictis. quaꝝ
quidem mantaꝝ illꝫ q estatis
tpr tenebūtur sint albe signiˢ
nris Regiis exornate. Alie vo
q yemis tpr tenebūtur sint ru
bee signis nris regiis cōmunite
Incip. vi. ps / de ordinatioib ad
offi. camlegor ⁊ eis subiectoꝝ ptī

De vestibꝰ et aliis ornamentis

Regalꝭ
prudentia /
cuncta benē
disponere cup
iens / summe
debet inten
dere / qꝫ in vestibꝰ et aliis ornā
mētis semper gestū suū / sup
fluitatē excessivaꝝ vestium
que potius ad fastū ascribitur
qꝫ ad laudem / pcipue repmen
to i ceteris ornamētis etiam
honestatem debitam obsūa
do / qꝫ eī laudabilius circa sta
tum principis reputatur qꝫ or
dinare gestū suū taliter qꝫ
gratus oibꝰ appeat ⁊ honestꝰ.

Directly under the miniature, a decorated initial confirms the interpretation given above: two menservants are carrying on their arms the clothes just ordered by the chamberlain. This initial, although painted by the artist of the large miniature, is entirely different in coloring: a certain blue and beige-ocher resemble the colors in favor with the Gothic miniaturists of central Europe, but even so, one feels the Southern influence. The golden balls, and the unfolded leaves at the end of the baguette are also in the Italian style. The checkered background of the initials looks rather French. It must be admitted that the burnished gold surfaces have neither the brightness nor the distinctness we admire in manuscripts of a comparable quality coming, for instance, from northern France.

From a stylistic point of view, these miniatures are reminiscent of the productions of northern Italy and, more precisely, of Siena. One should bear in mind, however, that the Italian manner had deeply influenced the northern and eastern coasts of the Mediterranean, from Catalonia to the Near East, and since James II of Majorca was also Count of Roussillon and Lord of Montpellier, he most probably employed artists from these areas, into which the Italian style had already penetrated. On the other hand, this circumstance would also account for some of the non-Italian features of these miniatures.

This copy of *The Palatine Laws* includes eight miniatures that occupy the whole width of the page; they correspond with the eight parts of the text. Each one of these is subdivided into a varied number of chapters beginning with an illuminated initial. The illumination reproduced here introduces the sixth part, which describes the duties of the chamberlain. One may notice in the title a tiny black ink abbreviation *rum*, added to the word *Camerlengo*, to correct the copyist's mistake.

The large frontispiece miniature, unfortunately badly damaged, represents King James II seated on his throne, attended by three bishops and by three gentlemen in armor. The coat of arms of Aragon, the country from which came this King of Majorca, and some shields of Queen Constance of Aragon, are painted in several places in the *Ordinances*. This was therefore the private copy belonging to the King James II who reigned over the Balearic Islands after 1423. *The Palatine Laws* date from 1337; this royal copy must have been made soon after, later than the *Book of Privileges*, that other very richly decorated manuscript written for the unfortunate king. Granted by James I the Conqueror to the people of Majorca, the *Book of Privileges* was written by Romeu des Poal in 1334; it is kept in the Archives of Majorca.

How can we account for the presence in the Royal Library of Belgium of the royal copy of *The Palatine Laws*? The story of this manuscript is just as hectic as that of the Peterborough Psalter. When James II was deprived of his kingdom of the Balearic Islands by Peter IV of Aragon, he sought refuge in France. Philip VI of Valois, instead of giving him assistance, compelled him to sell the county of Montpellier. While the bargaining was going on, James II offered the King of France his own copy of the *Ordinances*. Later, King John the Good gave it to his son Philip, duke of Burgundy. We might assume that this book would then enter the safe keeping of the "Library of Burgundy," but this was not the case. Isabella of Bourbon, second wife of Charles the Bold, presented William de la Baume, her knight of honor, with the precious manuscript. The latter had his coat of arms painted on the last page of the manuscript and signed it himself. From this private collection the copy came, one does not know how, into the hands of the Jesuits in Ruremond, then to their *Domus Professa* in Antwerp. When the Society was suppressed, this priceless copy of *The Palatine Laws* was returned to the "Library of Burgundy," only to be sent again to Paris, this time because of the French Revolution. The Congress of Vienna brought it back for the third time to Brussels.

## 13 The Crucifixion with the Virgin, St. John, and Donors

SO-CALLED MISSAL OF LOUIS DE MALE. *Southern Netherlands, possibly Brussels. Beginning of the second half of the fourteenth century.*
*217 folios ($14^3/_4 \times 11^1/_2$"); illustrations for the calendar; 12 historiated initials; 1 full-page miniature.*
*Ms. 9217, f. 115 v*

THIS CRUCIFIXION comes just before the Canon of the Mass and has no iconographic novelty deserving of special attention. But the originality displayed in the decoration of the whole page as well as the motifs have won this manuscript a choice place in the history of fourteenth-century illumination. This representation of Christ on the Cross does not conform to the German tradition, where we often see angels holding chalices to catch the blood as it flows from the wounds. The body of Christ as it hangs on the cross is drawn with all the gracefulness that a medieval artist could have given to figures and drapery at the beginning of the Gothic period. The figures of Mary and St. John are painted with elegance, but their hands and faces are not nearly so expressive as those of Christ. At the foot of the cross kneel a man and a woman of aristocratic birth who are, most certainly, the donors of this precious Missal. They are painted on a much smaller scale than the three main actors of the Passion drama. This is in accordance with a very old tradition we have seen before, which forbade the representing of human beings on the same scale as God or even His saints.

The impact of tradition also accounts for the portal that frames the central scene. This portal was certainly not required by the subject, since the Crucifixion took place on Golgotha; nor can it be considered as a conventional frame, for one already enframes the miniature, its four corner

medallions containing the symbols of the evangelists. It is, rather, a remnant of that realistic architectural background prevalent in antique art that we have seen, misshapen and misinterpreted during the Romanesque period (plates 6 & 8) and again, along new lines, in the early part of the Gothic age (plate 9). In this present case, the development of this ornamental process has reached what might be considered the baroque stage. The architectural design is dissipated in a mass of details – buttresses, niches, and turrets – which are quite unrealistic. The illuminator has even amused himself by painting human faces at the windows without considering their proportion to the buildings. Only later will the growing sensitiveness to reality temper such excesses of whim and fancy.

The background of the miniature shows a characteristic feature often encountered in English manuscripts of the first half of the fourteenth century and also, though much more seldom, on the Continent. The checkering, instead of being evenly spread on the whole background, is divided into four parts; these contain two different settings, arranged diagonally. The extremely linear style of the miniature is also borrowed from Insular manuscripts. The golden trilobate leaves around the margins are quite exceptional. In western Europe most manuscripts rather show a schematized vineleaf in their margin. This motif had found its way into the first manuscripts of the Gothic period and had been used more and more, until later illuminators started to introduce flowers, fruit, and an astounding variety of acanthus foliage. Unfortunately it has not yet been possible to trace the origin of the very unusual marginal detail, which we find again and again throughout the book. The lower part of the Crucifixion frame includes a cross, as is customary at this point of the missal. It is not the usual Latin cross, but this may be due to the illuminator's own fancy and not to any particular iconographic tradition.

In missals the most important miniature is always the Crucifixion, and those for whom the manuscript is intended are usually represented there. In this case, even the coats of arms of the owners were painted, but these have later been neatly covered with bands of blue squares on both sides of the miniature. Looking at the *recto* of this folio 115 it is easy to trace several shields beneath these bands. There is no doubt that they were the arms of the first owners; similar alterations can be traced in many other places in the book.

The predominance of beige and the lavish use of burnished, sometimes tooled gold (which is somewhat archaic if compared with the French manuscripts) are not the only exceptional techniques in this codex. We must also notice the very skillful preparation of the vellum with its elaborate system of ruling, the lovely mauve and red threadlike endings near the small initials, and some large letters with strange little monsters inside them. We find the latter from the end of the thirteenth century onward in tapestries, in frescoes, in the miniatures of western Germany along the Rhine and, later, in the manuscripts of the bishopric of Liège. The marginal decoration with large golden filets, and grotesques in which truculent Flemish proverbs are translated into pictures, adds the final touch to this beautiful and unusual book.

This Ms. 9217 is incorrectly called the Missal of Louis de Male because of the similarity of its style to that of Ms. 9427 of this same library, which is a breviary bearing this prince's coat of arms. Another manuscript equal in style and quality has reached us; it is Ms. 10.A.14 of the Royal Library in The Hague, a missal bearing on its last folio a very interesting colophon written in gold letters: there the illuminator, Laurent of Antwerp, a priest living in Ghent, declares that he finished his work on the book in 1366. Unfortunately, the miniatures in this Missal have been painted by noticeably different hands. Moreover, it has been even more altered than the Brussels Missal. It is therefore difficult to decide whether Laurent is the leader of the atelier and the actual artist of the Missal or whether he is only responsible for the repairs.

Neither does the liturgical use of the Brussels Missal help to solve the problem of its origin. The calendar is unquestionably for use in Liège and was therefore intended for someone belonging to that bishopric. On the other hand, since St. Gudula is named among the saints, we are led to think of Brussels as its place of origin. Another antiphonary belonging to the same group (Ms. 6926 of the Belgian Royal Library) was executed for the Benedictine Nuns of Forest, a suburb of Brabant's capital. This also points to the probable existence in Brussels, soon after the middle of the fourteenth century, of an important atelier of book illumination, which must have provided locally for such orders as those of the count of Flanders, and of a nobleman from the bishopric of Liège. The last word has yet to be said on this important question. Such a group of manuscripts, though it does not throw any new light on the history of Western illumination, presents an exceptionally luxurious type of book for the Low Countries in those days, which displays much originality in the use of foreign decorative features.

## 14 Farming in a "Good Democracy"

ARISTOTLE, Politics, *translated into French by Nicole Oresme. Paris. About 1372.*
*403 folios (8⅞ × 6"); 9 miniatures of various sizes; 2 full-page frontispiece miniatures facing each other.*
*Ms. 11201–2, f. 241*

UNDER THE TITLE "Good Democracy" that is written in the top margin, the illuminator has tried to keep as close as possible to the ideal conception of the text, as presented by the author. In this miniature two main subjects are brought together, whereas the other paintings in the book are generally divided into strips, each one containing a separate subject. It seems as if the painter were more at ease when he had to sketch agricultural work than he was when representing groups of people in conversation.

Rustic life is rendered with charm and sincerity. The horses have just stopped plowing and are having a rest; they stand aside, eating. The two drivers are also having their meal while another peasant is encouraging his horse to drag the harrow over the freshly plowed soil; a shepherd is looking after his sheep and playing the pipe. At the rear, men carrying tools are debating with each other. They seem to belong to two different groups; some wear a hood, others go bare-headed. The latter are certainly peasants. Their leader holds a kind of sickle in his hand and in both groups somebody is carrying a spade. Perhaps this is primarily a symbol for the concord that is supposed to reign in a "good democracy" by means of the fair exchange for opinions, problems, and responsibilities. The painter shows a real concern for composition. To give the illusion of depth, he makes clever use of a rather simple process: the figures are

Ci commence le sixte livre ou quel il determine de l'institution des especes de democracie & de olygarchie. et met les princeys ou offices des policies. et est aussi come perfection et acomplissement du quart livre. et contient viii chap.

Ou premier chap. Chap. Il propose son entencion.

Ou secont chapitre il met les suppositions & condicions et proprietez de democracie.

Ou tiers chapitre il traicte une question du droit de mocratique.

Ou quart il determine de quelles genz & de quelle maniere est la meilleur espece de democracie.

Ou quint. Chap. Il monstre par quelles loys

grouped along three separate planes. This effort at perspective goes only halfway, for the figures in the foreground are painted on the same scale as those in the rear. The general effect is reminiscent of the devices used in tapestry. On the other hand, the painter has skillfully drawn the shadows of the doors left open in the background building.

This page is probably the first representation in French painting of nature, not only because of the subject chosen but also in the technique of its composition. It is definitely a step forward. However, this lead will not be followed by everyone; even in the beginning of the fifteenth century, the artist of a number of miniatures which have been ascribed to the Master of Boucicaut could remain content with the showing of merely one or two rocks, a blue or starry sky, or even a checkered background. Here, we have a real landscape with an almost real horizon. The reason that there are so few imitators may be explained by a general lack of sensitiveness to the natural surroundings of life. The artists of those days had not yet discovered nature and were exclusively concerned with the doings of man himself; the exception noted here is apparently due to the text, which required a kind of illustration that obliged the painter to look around him. Books written on hunting, or such texts as the *Tacuinum Sanitatis*, provoked the same results. In this respect, the art of tapestry may also have paved the way, being a reflection of Italian paintings which were far closer to reality.

The representation of the human face has not progressed in the same way, for all figures are alike and merely linear. But the clothing and the draperies are remarkably modeled and, though some gestures remind us of a puppet show, the whole picture is so lively that one is captivated by its charm.

From the pictorial aspect, the general procedure is a compromise between grisaille and color, the figures being painted in grisaille, with a few touches of color in the face, for instance, while the background is almost monochrome.

The mushroom-like tree at the rear was for a long time considered the signature of an illuminator who was for this reason called the "Boqueteau Master." Now we know that this type of tree was very fashionable among illuminators, the idea emanating from France. In this miniature the trees are drawn with a refinement which suggests that they were the work of the best Paris workshop, the atelier of the Louvre, as it should be called. The features of the manuscript are also very refined: the baguette with its foliage scrolls and vignettes, the initials with their alternate coloring and their amazingly delicate threadlike endings, the script in perfect Gothic hand, without stiffness and excessive angularity. We owe to Raoulet d'Orléans the transcription of the *Politics*. He signed his name on the first page. A dozen manuscripts showing the same quality of handwriting can be ascribed to this master, who was probably also responsible for the other technical aspects pertaining to the execution of these books. He was certainly aided in his work by numerous collaborators who were required to conform strictly to his style.

This kind of manuscript is typical of the reign of Charles V of France; the contents of the text alone are sufficient proof of this. The work of Aristotle had not been very long in use in the universities when the king ordered this translation, and we know of no other French translation in existence during the Middle Ages. The appreciation of such a text testifies to the monarch's wide knowledge and eager interest in cultural matters; we owe the quality of the text to a really enlightened bibliophile.

This copy of the *Politics* bears no coat of arms but it is difficult to believe that it would not have been ordered by the king himself. It belonged to the Louvre library from whence it went, in 1425, to the Duke of Bedford, at that time Governor of Paris and a great collector of books. It is probably through his wife, who was the sister of Philip the Good, that the manuscript finally came to rest in the "Library of Burgundy," where it is mentioned in the inventory of 1467.

## 15 Emperor Charles IV and the Seven Electors

GELRE, Armorial. Geldern. *About 1370 with numerous later additions. 124 folios ($8^5/_8 \times 5^1/_2$"); 2 full-page miniatures; many coats of arms. Ms. 15652–56, f. 26*

SINCE THIS MINIATURE is at the beginning of an armorial of the German Empire, it is safe to assume that these eight personages represent the Emperor of Germany and the seven Electors. Indeed, the section of the manuscript devoted to the *Armorial* comprises first the Emperor's shield with helmet and crest, then, on a smaller scale, the numerous blazons of his closer attendants with their names. Following this come the seven Electors, three ecclesiastics and four laymen, each with his own shield. The Electors' shields are accompanied by many smaller ones pertaining to vassals.

From the contents of the manuscript it is possible to infer that the *Armorial* dates back to about 1370, thus allowing us to identify each member of the group. In the middle of the painting is seated Emperor Charles IV wearing his crown and a mantle thrown over his armor; he holds in his hands the sword and the globe of his rank. The three ecclesiastical Electors are: the Archbishop of Mainz, John of Luxemburg; the Archbishop of Trier, Cuno of Falkenstein; and the Archbishop of Cologne, Frederick of Saarwerden. On the Emperor's left we recognize his son Wenceslas, king of Bohemia; Robert I, count Palatine of the Rhine; Wenceslas, duke of Saxony; and Otto V, margrave of Brandenburg.

Some object to this identification on the basis that two of the so-called lay Electors, the larger

figures on the extreme right of the miniature, are dressed in a way unsuitable to their dignity. It has therefore been suggested that they are a bourgeois and a peasant who, together with the King of Bohemia, represent the three social classes of the Empire. The small figure in the foreground would be Gelre, the herald himself. This suggestion is worth considering. It is of importance to know, for instance, if the necklace he wears in this picture is that of a herald. But would it not seem strange that a peasant should be painted at that time on the frontispiece miniature of such a manuscript?

An armorial is a book meant for frequent reference, but such a miniature, even though it were a frontispiece, was not likely to be looked at very often. Its subject would most probably have been treated with more care if the painting concerned was intended to be constantly under the eye of its owner or his attendants. In any case, the painter does not seem to have worried a great deal about his drawing.

This page is nevertheless a landmark in the history of illumination, showing a new tendency in art manifested by a truer representation of the human form. The faces are almost portraits. Such an achievement is seldom encountered during this period in so unpretentious a work. The figure drawing, however, presents undeniable defects: the emperor's feet and knees are clumsy and the clerics' gestures are all alike. It is fascinating to compare this effort with delicate Parisian miniatures, which, as late as the early fifteenth century, still had not succeeded (except perhaps in a few masterpieces) in rendering the individuality of faces, even in works destined for royal use. Here the personal features are remarkably well differentiated, especially those of the four princes.

The name of Malouel, or Maelwel, has been suggested as the executant of this large drawing. He may have been practicing his art in his own country of Gelder before he started building up his fame in Paris. In any case a miniature such as this one may be considered a brilliant forerunner of the striking innovations of the Dutch miniaturists of the fifteenth century, insofar as they express the same profoundly human values.

The manuscript has other claims to our admiration. It is certainly one of the most beautiful medieval armorials to have been preserved. Several pages are dedicated to the many kingdoms and princedoms of the day, including their feudal hierarchy, as well as to the Emperor, the seven Electors, and their vassals. Such data was indispensable for the herald of any mighty prince and one can well imagine how useful this book is for the history of the Middle Ages.

The *Armorial* begins with a collection of poems in Dutch, which are essential for the history of that literature. These poems consist of pieces of verse either in the epic style or with a historical character: challenges to John III, duke of Brabant, rhymed chronicles of the dukes of Brabant and of the counts of Flanders, or poems in praise of valorous knights. In one of these texts we discover the author's name: Gelre, for the country of which he was the herald. It is not impossible, though no evidence can be given, that he himself may have written the texts and even painted the numerous coats of arms in the *Armorial*, since his duties may not have been sufficiently important to allow him to employ a professional scribe-illuminator. The poems are all in the same hand but were not written at the same time. The handwriting is so uniform, though, that the transcription must have been carried on at comparatively short intervals.

From the documents available in the Archives we know that Gelre was in charge as herald under Reinalt II, Reinalt III and Eduard, who was married to Catherine of Bavaria and died in 1371. We do not know if Gelre remained in office under William of Juliers, who married Eduard's widow. Nor can we be certain that Gelre was the same as a certain "Beyeren quondam Gelre" who signed a *Chronicle of Holland* (Brussels Ms. 17914) in 1401.

It is generally admitted that the impressive work of the herald of the Duke of Gelder was begun around 1370 and that it was undertaken to satisfy the needs of heraldic illustrations as well as poetic inspiration.

# 16 Charles V of France as Patron of the Sciences

ARISTOTLE, Ethics, *translated into French by Nicole Oresme. Paris. About 1376. 224 folios (12 1/2 × 8 1/2"); 9 small miniatures; 2 large miniatures with several panels.*
*Ms. 9505–6, f. 2 v*

AS A MATTER of principle at least, during the Middle Ages, kings were supposed to be the patrons of letters and fine arts. This role became the subject matter of numerous miniatures in which kings were painted receiving a book from the hands of its author. Not only do the four miniatures represented here emphasize this traditional theme, but also they attest a keen and personal interest on this French monarch's part.

In the first panel, Charles V is seated on a throne surrounded by high curtains. A scholar, on one knee, presents a manuscript; the king, bending slightly from his throne, accepts the proffered gift. His attitude and his gesture of welcome show a genuine benevolence, further enhanced by the kindly expression on his face. A third character, peeping from behind the curtain, is keeping an eye on the whole scene; it is somewhat difficult to guess what he is doing there. Perhaps it is simply a device suggesting the king's simple habits in his private life. We notice, besides, that the king does not wear his crown but a sort of cap which is very similar to the headgear of the university professors.

In the second section, the king and queen are seated, each wearing a crown: the king on his throne, with two little boys standing slightly behind him, and the queen on a kind of pedestal, with a little girl almost hidden from view. The boys and the girl are doubtless their own

il propose la fin & le finit de ceste science · oeuvres · côme une maison ou un vaissel

Tout art et toute doctrine · et semblablement tout fait ou operacion et eleccion appetent & desirent aucun bien · pour ce parloient bien les anciens en disant ainsi · bië est ce q̃ toutes chos · desirent.

Et semble que il est difference de fins · car les unes fins sont les operacions · les autres sont aucunes oeuvres · ou choses faites hors les operacions ou facons · et ces oeuvres sõt meilleurs

children: Charles VI, the future King of France, Louis, duke of Orléans, whom John the Fearless murdered in 1407, and Catherine. The royal couple are carrying on a discussion, perhaps even an argument, over the children: the queen, Joanna of Bourbon, is lifting her hands in sign of protest. The king, while looking toward his wife, points his finger at the two children standing behind him. This gesture may be interpreted as the sign of some decision taken by the father, of which the mother does not approve.

The next panel of the miniature depicts a lecture at the university; a lecturer is commentating on the text of a volume lying open on a stand. It may be Nicole Oresme himself, who translated Aristotle's works, lecturing on the Greek philosopher. The listeners, who are all adults, are sitting behind straight desks, on which they keep their books open to follow the text. The king is among them, in the first row. He wears a crown and the same sort of white band on his mantle that we see him wearing in the other part of the miniature. The significance of this scene is obvious; we could have no better proof of the monarch's intellectual aspirations.

The subject of the last panel is more intricate: on the right, another lecture is in progress, given this time by a teacher in a classroom. On the doorstep, a man holding a long stick seems to be pushing a frightened child toward his father or tutor. It may be, on the contrary, that the child is being introduced by his tutor to the schoolmaster and is showing his fear of the stick.

In spite of possible differences in the interpretation of details we may assume that the four pictures illustrate a whole program of education: after having read Aristotle's *Ethics*, given to him by Nicole Oresme himself, the king decides he will have his children educated. In order to make up for the deficiencies of his own learning, he resumes his place on the university benches and submits his elder son to the strict discipline of the school. It must be remembered that the King of France had himself ordered this translation of the Greek philosopher; furthermore he had asked that a private copy should be made by his scribes and illuminators. We must go back to St. Louis to find, in France, a sovereign whose interest was so personal and efficient.

This copy of the *Ethics* is not a small-size manuscript, like the *Politics* (plate 14), but a luxurious book. The setting of the page has reached the stage of perfection; its rulings are so skillfully adjusted that they never fail to mark the difference between the text and its gloss. Both are written in the same style, but the gloss is on a smaller scale. We recognize the hand, or rather the manner, of Raoulet d'Orléans, the scribe of the *Politics* and probably the leader of the Louvre atelier. It is not necessary to dwell afresh on the beauty of this handwriting, though its merits tend to pass unnoticed, so fascinated are we by the exceptional quality of the whole page. Each and every one of its aspects are equally perfect in technique: the exquisitely refined, threadlike endings, the initials in the purest Gothic style containing vignettes rich in gold and color, the marginal decoration also truly Gothic, with its graceful foliage ornaments supported by a baguette. In the margins, too, we find some of those very sophisticated grotesques that flourished in the days of Jean Pucelle and remain linked with his name: human busts carried by an incredible variety of animals' feet, or busts protruding from a border decoration.

The technique of the miniature shows a definite improvement on that of the *Politics* (plate 14). This appears first of all in the coloring where we find a beautiful range of tints, instead of grisaille and monochrome backgrounds. Movements are more expressive and faces more individual, there is also a greater consciousness of the human soul and its sentiments. This progress is most apparent in the panel showing the royal family.

We regret the total absence of landscape, though it might be argued that it is somewhat alien to the subject. The illuminator was content with the usual background, either decorated with fleurs-de-lis or checkered, and arranged diagonally. The architectural style of the miniature, which gives it an air of dignity, is set off by a quadrilobe in three colors that encloses each panel. This tricolored pattern, which first appeared at the time of Charles V, is as good as a signature for determining the origin of manuscripts in which it is found. After the king's death in 1380, this fashion died out rapidly and had entirely disappeared by the beginning of the fifteenth century.

We find in the foreword a statement by Nicole Oresme to the effect that he finished his translation in 1370. We should not be too hasty in ascribing our copy to that date, for Charles V had another one made in a smaller size and similar in all ways to the *Politics*, but dated 1376 (Ms. 10. D.1 in the Meerman Museum, The Hague). The two transcriptions could be contemporary. A careful archaeological examination might solve the problem, provided it covered not only the two manuscripts in Brussels and The Hague, but also a luxury copy of the *Politics* belonging to the collection of the Count de Wazier.

The miniature represented here belongs to the copy which was the result of the collaboration of several artists. To give any precise idea of the part played by each one of them would, again, need an archaeological investigation of all the other manuscripts coming from the same center during the same period. In fact these productions are all strikingly alike, a drawback due to the protection granted by the king to whom, in all other respects, the art of the illumination owes so much. At no other moment in its history did Parisian illumination maintain such a high standard of perfection.

17

# Christ Enthroned Surrounded by the Symbols of the Four Evangelists

MISSAL OF SAINTE-CHAPELLE, PARIS. *Paris. About 1400.*
*525 folios (15¾ × 11¼"); 2 full-page miniatures facing each other; 27 historiated initials.*
*Ms. 9125, f. 178*

ONCE ISOLATED from the rest of the manuscript, this page, because of its most unusual style, would be difficult to ascribe to any particular center of production. Since its original size had to be reduced to the format of this present volume, it is less easy to tell what type of book it was meant to illustrate. The general aspect is really grandiose in spite of the many weaknesses in the drawing which appear when examined at close quarters.

Christ appears as a thick-set figure seated on an abnormally wide throne. Why did the artist draw his central character so as to cover almost the whole width of the miniature? Why these vast draperies and outspread knees? The answer probably lies in the requirements of the composition. It also seems as if the painting were a rough transposition of some sculpture in wood. As for the front part of the throne, it may have been given this width in order to enhance the perspective by means of contrast. There is no example in other miniatures of any throne with so few ornamental decorations and architectural motifs. The throne was usually a very elaborate construction in French and Italian miniatures. An interesting comparison could be made, in this respect, with the Virgin's throne in the *Belles Heures de Jean de Berry* (plate 20).

The arms, and more still the hands with such awkward fingers, are heavy, like the lower part of the body; the gesture of holding the banner unfurled on the top of the sphere also lacks

grace. The face of Our Lord, however, looks so very human, with its strongly marked features and loose hair, that it makes a strong contrast to more conventional representations of Christ painted around 1400.

The composition of this page was evidently a matter of concern for the artist; this appears in the way he has fitted the symbols of the evangelists into the spaces left by the central figure, saving two wide triangles at the top and a strip at the bottom. This has provided him with ample space for the angel on the left, as well as for the scroll in the angel's hands. He also has space to unfurl further down, on the right, the scroll caught in the eagle's beak and claws. The winged lion and bull stand in the lower part of the picture. More details confirm the artist's horror of unused space: the two receding corners at the base of the throne allow for the bull's wings and for the lion's tail, which is so long as to be almost ridiculous, while the eagle's scroll follows the curves of the banner held by Christ.

The checkered ground, which was a twelfth-century innovation, reached its zenith in French illumination with its various and attractive formulations of golden and colored squares, often decorated with white filigree. Seldom has this technique achieved such brilliance as in this page: it is almost incredible that so many tiny squares should have been painted with such perfect regularity by a human hand.

The marginal decoration is usually looked upon as the signature of the atelier where the miniature was made; in this case it is so special that it can be ascribed to no known workshop, since there is no other book with a margin decorated with six-pointed stars. The delicate arrangement of the scroll pattern bearing these stars, and the presence of columbines, are the only clues which lead us to think of France, and even of Paris, as the origin of this superb manuscript. The other decoration to be found in the margin is the cross which is only partly visible in this plate. This page, standing in the missal at the Canon, is here in addition to the usual Crucifixion, and is facing it. By comparison with other missals, such as that of Louis de Male, the very fact of an addition of this size, in that place, proves the desire to make an exceptional decoration for this book.

Only a very special destination can explain such wealth of illustration. The calendar of the Missal, written in blue and gold letters, gives full support to this assertion. Liturgical use in Paris is implied by the selection of saints. With other important information, we learn that the Sainte-Chapelle was dedicated on the 26th of April: *Dedicatio Capellae Regis parisiensis.* The Missal was therefore intended for the royal chapel, which accounts for its beauty.

The five hundred folios of the manuscript have been copied in the most exquisite Gothic script. Its impressive bulk is due to the large number of texts accompanied by musical staves, drawn with all the refinement one would expect to find in a book of this quality. The marginal decoration shows everywhere the same very unusual star motif that has been observed around this Christ enthroned.

The seventeen historiated initials seem all to be made by the same brush and in the same manner as the two large miniatures; they have been painted with almost as much care. The contrast is thus striking between all the secondary decorative techniques of the Missal and its illustrations: while the preparation of the pages is exquisitely refined and displays a perfect mastery in the art of making books, the style of the illustrative vignettes, though strong and expressive, is clumsy and inexperienced. We know of no other work by this master, but we venture to suggest that it was done by a foreign artist, possibly from southern Germany, who still painted in the style of his own country. It is likely that in this case a foreigner would lose some of his native stylistic vigor through daily contact with the delicate craftmanship of his French colleagues. They, in turn, would acquire from him something of his vigorous style. It was by such exchanges that the art of illumination in Paris unceasingly renewed itself during the Gothic period.

An additional notice in the calendar mentions the funeral of Michel de Creney, who died in 1409; he had been Bishop of Auxerre and chaplain to Charles VI, king of France. The Missal was therefore made shortly before that time since we can approximately date the marginal decoration, thanks to its density and to the presence of the columbines. Moreover, the manuscript was already mentioned in the inventory made for Philip the Good in 1420. Was it given to him by Charles VI himself before he died in 1422, or is it just another case of plundering the Louvre library during one of the periods of insanity that afflicted the unfortunate French monarch?

# 18 The Circumcision

GUILLAUME DE DIGULEVILLE, The Pilgrimage of the Life of Man; The Pilgrimage of the Soul; *and* The Pilgrimage of Jesus Christ. *France. Possibly about 1400.*
*300 folios (9 × 5⁷/₈"); 113 miniatures in various sizes; 1 large double-page miniature.*
*Ms. 10176–78, f. 222*

AMONG THE SCENES illustrating the childhood of Christ, the Circumcision is not often chosen to be reproduced. It does not belong, strictly speaking, to the cycle of the eight subjects selected for the Hours of the Virgin. In almost all the books of hours, the feast of the Circumcision and that of the Presentation in the Temple are combined in the same picture, and as a result of this iconographic tradition, Simeon not only receives the child, presented by his parents with the usual offerings, but he also performs the operation. This miniature, however, shows a total disregard for this convention; we shall see that its originality is expressed further in its aesthetic merits.

The Child occupies the center of the picture, but His figure is on a more massive scale than that of the other characters. His half-seated, half-lying position seems to have been copied from a model in which He was supported by His mother or resting in her arms. But here, Mary is out of reach of her Son and is on the point of rising from her couch in protest against the painful rite; her hands remain contracted, expressing in a pathetic way a mother's grief at the sight of the suffering inflicted on her son. Only Joseph's face is visible behind Mary; it shows no emotion, but it is full of character. However, it is the group of three women at the right that displays the artist's talent and originality at their best. The first thing that we will notice is

that the operation is performed by a woman. This detail is enough to deprive the rite of its liturgical character; it is as if this were the village midwife who normally performed with such duties. The painter has made no effort to convince us that she is practicing her craft with any refinement or with the slightest sympathy for the child she is about to hurt; on the contrary, to make sure that she remains unaffected by the Virgin's tormented gesture, the second woman shows her approval by patting her on the back to encourage her, while throwing a contemptuous look at the wretched parents. The third woman has the face of a brute; on her weird countenance is a mixture of curiosity and indifference.

The miniature, as we shall soon see, was painted, like the rest of the manuscript, about 1400 – in any case, not later than the beginning of the fifteenth century. One would search in vain through the whole history of European painting of this period to find another artist so bold as to render familiarly an event that had previously been considered sacred. Our illuminator's originality is shown also by the vigor and variety of the sentiments he expresses. He is ahead of his contemporaries in this respect, since he contrives to make the faces look more human; he is even a whole century ahead, in that he paints ugly faces and obviously enjoys the horrible. The picture described above is not the only illustration in the *Three Pilgrimages* in this style. The manuscript comprises about a hundred miniatures by the same hand, all displaying the same qualities, though not always the same vigor. However, they are never trivial. A few examples will give a better idea of this artist who has remained too long unknown. Hell is represented as a crater where monstrous devils are inflicting the most terrible torments on the damned. The following miniature makes use of a process quite uncommon in the Middle Ages but very much in favor nowadays: it consists in reproducing a detail of the previous picture on a larger scale. In the enlargement, the devils are prodding with their forks the bodies of their victims which hang in atrocious positions on the long arm of a gibbet. Though he is more at ease in the exceptional and the dramatic, our artist can convey his particular vision of reality even in the usual iconography. One of the most poignant is the crucified Christ whose body is entirely painted in green, thus enhancing the pathetic effect of the drawing with the coloring.

Strangely enough, the painter combines these stylistic qualities, really unique for his time, with the most rudimentary technical processes. The colors are flat and weak, pervaded by a greenish shade tinged with gray that makes the whole painting look slovenly and sometimes even dirty. The pigment he uses is not like the usual gouache; it looks like an almost transparent watercolor wash applied with large strokes of the brush. The drawing, however, is very firm. This, combined with the artist's talent for choosing original subjects, and his excellent compositions, compels our admiration. Our illuminator had something to tell and he tells it in such a way that, in spite of his poor technique, his work is one of the most original in medieval painting. He can be compared to one painter only: the Master of the Hours of Rohan, whose message was very akin but who attained, in his best pages at least, a more classical achievement, while losing none of his vigor.

One finds only very few elements in the manuscript which help one to establish the origin of the Master of the *Three Pilgrimages*. This copy of Diguleville's work was intended for a Benedictine monk belonging to the illustrious family of Guisnes, from Artois, whose coat of arms appears on the last miniature. A person of his importance might have received the book as a gift, or ordered it from any workshop. The manuscript as a whole, however, is very French in style; it might even have been made in Paris, for the most minute details have been treated with the utmost care. Technical aspects and the background pattern of the miniatures enable us to date it around 1400, whereas the few landscapes of rocks surmounted by a tree indicate more exactly the fashion prevailing in the early years of the fifteenth century.

As for the pictures themselves, we do not feel inclined to ascribe them to a French artist. If this painter had been a Parisian, the manuscript would not have been the only one of its kind. As in the Sainte-Chapelle Missal (plate 17), the possibility of a German painter is not excluded. The hard drawing and the rough treatment of low quality pigments would indicate the Upper Rhine.

This volume has only recently interested art critics. The history of illumination had been too long confined to the study and reproduction of the very refined manuscripts executed for the great princes. Nowadays the student of illumination has widened his horizons. The Master of the *Three Pilgrimages*, if he ever worked in Paris, must have shocked the people around him, but he probably paved the way in public opinion for the more moderate realism of his followers: the three Limbourg brothers.

19–20

# Jean de Berry Presented to the Madonna by His Two Patron Saints

LES BELLES HEURES DE JEAN DE FRANCE, DUC DE BERRY, *also called* LES TRÈS BELLES HEURES OF BRUSSELS. *Paris. Beginning of the fifteenth century.*
*276 folios (10¾ × 11¼"); 17 historiated initials; 20 full-page miniatures with marginal decoration; 2 large corresponding miniatures on a double page.*
*Ms. 11060–61, ff. 10 and 11*

THE HISTORY of medieval illumination has only some rare specimens to show of a single subject distributed on two pages facing each other. It is better to reproduce them in their original presentation and not as they are generally reproduced, separately or one after the other. This composite miniature is, with the frontispiece of the *Chroniques de Hainaut* (plate 27), doubtless the best-known possession of the "Library of Burgundy." The book from which it is taken should not, under any circumstances, be confused with *Les Très Riches Heures du Duc de Berry*, preserved in the Condé Museum in Chantilly.

In the center of the left-hand page is Jean de Berry, the brother of Charles V of France and of Philip the Bold, duke of Burgundy; he wears an ermine cape and is kneeling at a prie-dieu on which lies an open prayer book. We have here an authentic portrait of this great French prince and insatiable collector of works of art, whose characteristic features – receding forehead and thick-set jaws – are recognizable in several other portraits, sometimes in profile, sometimes full face. The clever rendering of such an unusual face contrasts with the rigidity of the hands; their conventional gesture is typical of an attitude that is often wrongly called the donor's, because it is usually, at least where manuscripts are concerned, the attitude of the person for whom the book was intended. These donors, represented kneeling in prayer, are sometimes painted alone, without any representation either of God, the Virgin, or the saints. Here, however, the artist's intention to paint his subject as a diptych is evident from the presence of the duke's patron saints, who seem to be presenting Jean de Berry to the Madonna and Child. The Apostle Andrew's protective gesture cannot be interpreted otherwise; John the Baptist is placing his hand on the duke's shoulder, but his intention is not so clearly expressed. These attitudes attest that the miniature on the right-hand page is the necessary complement of that on the left. Nevertheless, the position of the two patron saints is harder to understand in relation to the kneeling duke and the seated Madonna; the artist has been compelled to represent St. Andrew and St. John half-kneeling, half-standing, to raise them a little above their protégé. John the Baptist does not cut a very successful figure in his attempt to bend his knee; his half-lifted foot is probably due to faulty perspective. On the other hand, his eyes are turned toward the prince and his look is so lively that we have the feeling that we have come in at the very moment he was turning around to introduce him to the Madonna. The saints' faces cannot be said to have the charm of portraits, but they are so profoundly human that they entirely satisfy our imagination.

A Madonna of the type called "à la supplique" fills the miniature on the facing page. She is suckling the Child Jesus, who has just stopped taking the breast and seems to turn His eyes toward the kneeling figure. He is holding a pen in His right hand and writes on a long scroll which coils under Mary's right hand. She holds the other end of the scroll in her left while keeping two fingers free to support the Child. Her fingers are disproportionate and the movement of her arms is unnatural; but the sense of observation displayed here by the artist goes far beyond that of any contemporary painter or illuminator. In the beginning of the fifteenth century attempts to represent a complex series of movements with accuracy were most rare. The Child's attitude is just as bold. He is sitting on His mother's knee with one leg hanging down and the other one folded on her lap, thus showing the sole of His foot; here again, our illuminator shows his exceptional gift for innovation.

In current usage, the Child Jesus in the Madonna "à la supplique" is supposed to be writing down on the scroll His favorable answer to the donor's prayer. Sometimes the scroll is linking the donor to Jesus and His mother. In these pages the subject has lost its meaning, perhaps because there are two miniatures. Why also is there no text at all on this scroll, when the illuminator took such trouble to write in very small script on the background scrolls of this miniature: *Gloria in Excelsis* and *Ave gratia plena*?

The great merits of this beautiful page do not prevent us, however, from noticing its undeniable weaknesses. One of the most conspicuous is the foreshortening of the Madonna's right leg, which is completely unrealistic. The head is by no means perfect either, as one cheek appears

smaller than the other. This mistake has perhaps the advantage of giving individuality to the face. Moreover, the monumental form of the throne is not justified; the arches surmounting the two arms of the seat, and the columns at the lower part, are superfluous. How far we are from the Gothic spirit, which always remained functional, even when it was overdecorated and decadent!

The most legitimate criticism, however, cannot impair the beauty conveyed by these two pictures. This reaction is probably due, first of all, to the extraordinarily refined technique of the grisaille that enabled the artist to render the most precise and delicate details. We are struck at first glance by the neat and undulating folds of the draperies that the artist seems to have multiplied for the mere sake of practicing his skill, and we cannot but admire the fine modeling of the faces.

We still do not know whom to credit with these two pages, which are among the best works of medieval illumination. For a long time it was believed that they could be ascribed to Jacquemart de Hesdin, because the Book of Hours which they accompany was allegedly the work of this illuminator. We know from documents that the talent of this artist was certainly great, but his style has not yet been identified for certain. These two pages have been added to the Hours, and were not originally part of them. They are of a much larger format and, moreover, the Book of Hours has a presentation miniature that condenses into one painting the two pages described here. We are thus confined to mere suppositions that would be too long to develop here. These two pages were probably the greatest work of the artist, that into which he put his best effort. We can, of course, hope to find his hand again elsewhere but it might be less individualized and perhaps even already adapted to the manner of his collaborators. Besides, if he were gifted – and who would deny that he was? – he may have altered and improved his style. Is it therefore too daring to claim the Christ Enthroned from the Sainte-Chapelle Missal (plate 17) as one of the early works of this master?

The marginal decorations on both these pages are so original and, from a historical point of view, so important, that they deserve further comment. They are encountered only in the books that Jean de Berry ordered for himself, for the prince not only summoned the best among his painters, but also expected them to display originality even in the borders of his books. This decoration shows three distinctive features: first, it makes no use of the vine leaf which was the motif current after the first quarter of the century; in its place, we have a few natural flowers such as columbines and a large number of conventionalized flowers, interspersed with different kinds of birds and, here and there, butterflies. All these ornaments spring from a central stem, a process never encountered in genuine Parisian marginal decoration. Barbed quatrefoils decorate the angles and are also distributed regularly along the central baguette. These particular ornaments, obviously coming from Italy, were intended to enshrine blazons or other heraldic motifs. Four emblems belonging to Jean de Berry are distributed with perfect symmetry around the two pages: his well-known coat of arms, an azure field strewn with golden lilies; the wounded swan (*le cygne navré*); a bear; and two interlaced initials: a *V* (or *U*) with an *E*. King René d'Anjou, when referring to Jean de Berry in his book *Livre du cœur d'amours épris*, mentions this coat of arms; he does not explain the bear, but he recounts that the duke had adopted the wounded white swan in remembrance of a love affair he had had in England when, together with his father, he was there held captive: *Pour elle prins un mot et mis soulz mon escu le cygne blanc navré, autre mot plus n'y fut* (For her sake I choose a motto and put a white wounded swan under my escutcheon; other motto I nevermore had). But King René does not tell us what that motto was; neither does he quote the device *Le temps venra* (Time will come) that we find in some of the other manuscripts belonging to Jean de Berry. The feminine name of Ursine has been brought forward because it would be closely connected with the bear as an emblem and would provide the interlaced *U* and *E* as its first and last letters; but there is no conclusive evidence of this hypothesis.

We have already said that these two pages were independent of the manuscript they actually adorn. They could have been meant either to be included in a different book, or to be framed together as a real picture, like some other examples that are preserved today. But the marginal decoration and the white space left between the two pictures do not give much support to this suggestion.

The Book of Hours in which the two paintings are found is incomplete, like almost all the important works undertaken for the Duke of Berry. The calendar is missing and we find no antiphony that indicates any particular worship. There are some interruptions in the decoration: two miniatures, different in style and in coloring from the rest of the work, have been inserted into the book, and one of these has altered the original composition in a very noticeable way. Agreement is far from having been reached on the date and authorship of the miniatures. It is generally accepted that they display quite a large variety of styles considering the comparatively small number of pages which display a painting. On the other hand, the manuscript, because of its general decoration, is certainly very different from all other books made at that time.

21

# The Creation and Fall of the Angels

HISTORIATED BIBLE OF GUIARD DES MOULINS, *first part. Paris. About 1410.*
*435 folios (18 × 11¾"); 1 large frontispiece miniature with marginal decoration; 110 smaller miniatures.*
*Ms. 9001, f. 19*

THE SIX PICTURES assembled here show a development of the illustration of the prologue written in 1291 by Guiard des Moulins for his Historiated Bible. To understand its meaning. one must bear in mind that this large miniature comes before the Book of Genesis, in which each day of the Creation has its story decorated, according to custom, with a small miniature. Before linking this multiform illustration with the others, we must analyze it in detail.

The six sections of this folio should be read in the following order: first the three on the left, then the three on the right. In the first one, a woman wearing a blue garment and a mantle lined with ermine is seated on a large throne; she wears a crown and holds a scepter in her left hand. We have already noticed elsewhere (plate 17, Christ Enthroned, from the Sainte-Chapelle Missal) that the requirements of the composition induced the illuminator to broaden the throne, This necessity is even more apparent in this first picture, because it shows only one character whereas the five other scenes have at least three each. To fill the vacant space, the lower part of the throne forms a kind of platform, which has been exaggeratedly broadened in comparison with the back of the seat. This has been done at the expense of the perspective, to adjust the vertical figure to the horizontal schema imposed by the division of the whole picture. Moreover, we observe in this monumental throne architectural excesses similar to those already deplored in the Madonna "à la supplique" from the Hours of Jean de Berry (plate 20).

The regally clad occupant of this throne holds in her right hand a phylactery which unfurls itself all around her. It is perfectly legible: *Ab initio et ante secula, creata sum* (I was created

ab inicio et ante secula
creata sum
ascendam in celum

since the beginning and before time). As this text cannot possibly be applied to Mary, the mother of Christ, this woman must personify Divine Wisdom.

In the second picture, three characters are having a discussion. Their faces are alike, their robes and mantles are of the same color. All three have halos, but that of the middle figure is cruciform. It is obvious that they represent the Holy Trinity, though a problem arises when we start to identify them. The cruciform halo usually belongs to the Son who here is standing in the center, the usual place of the Father. Could it be just a mistake of the painter? The three Persons of the Trinity are carrying on a very lively conversation; one does not easily find, in the miniatures of that time, such a vivid depiction of people conversing together. The third picture illustrates the creation of the angels; the three divine Persons, in varying attitudes, all have the same gesture, blessing the angels they have just created.

While the first section is made of three distinctly separate pictures, the three following are closely related. In the top one are the Father, the Son, and the Holy Ghost, all wearing the same clothing as in the previous picture, and sitting on a long seat covered with a bright red cloth embroidered with flowers. The Father is barefoot, which is very unusual in the iconography of the Middle Ages. All three are sadly pointing to what is going on below in the fifth miniature, where Lucifer, painted in rich vermilion, is rising from the circle of archangels. The archdemon wears a crown and his overbearing pride is proclaimed on the scroll he holds in his hand: *Ascendam in coelum* (I will ascend into Heaven). Some of the angels turn away, terrified. Others who took the side of the rebel are thrust into hell; one of them, still clad in white, is falling down into the abyss; his arms are stretched downward, overlapping the gold frame which separates the miniatures. We come now to the last picture: Hell is represented as a huge monster blowing flames through its wide-open mouth that is directed upward to swallow the rebels; we can see Satan falling, his crowned head downward. Other angels, whose bright colors have vanished, have hands and feet now changed into claws.

This intricate iconography which describes the creation and fall of the angels is a necessary complement to the description in the Book of Genesis of the great drama of the Creation, since it comes prior to that text. This polyptych could be something besides a mere series of miniatures: one wonders, indeed, if the artist was not inspired by the mystery plays of the middle ages, in which the events of the Christian drama were explained in simple, understandable language.

The warm, sometimes even bold coloring, the elaborate composition, and the delicate softness of the drawing show evidence of the unusual skill of this master illuminator, to whom several other miniatures in the Historiated Bible may be ascribed. Only quite recently has his personality begun to arouse interest, although not to the extent of his merits. This shows how ignorant we are of the history of illumination in one of its most glorious moments: the Paris school at the turning point of the fourteenth and fifteenth centuries. This artist is, admittedly, eclipsed by such masters as Jacquemart de Hesdin, the Limbourg brothers, the Master of Boucicaut, and the Master of Rohan. But so talented an artist was certainly bound to have taken an important part in this new interest in illumination. Being the principal decorator of the manuscript, he deserves to be called the Master of the Historiated Bible of Brussels.

The marginal decoration of the page is typically French, with its ornamental foliage of vine leaves. Spaces have been left free so as to paint in monsters and birds; there is also a butterfly. The style of these vignettes is a little loose and shows less refinement than the rest of the border. Acanthus leaves and golden balls decorate the long baguette which frames the page. The origin of these motifs is certainly not French: they were borrowed from Italy, perhaps by way of Avignon. We realize that they had not yet been assimilated into the French fashion and must therefore show evidence of a foreign contribution in its primitive form, of which we have encountered several examples in preceding works. In any case, these motifs are never found elsewhere than on the frontispiece page, which is generally decorated with more care.

We may also find in our Historiated Bible a precious piece of information concerning the execution of medieval books. In the white filigrees on the purple and blue line endings, we discover in several places the words *Petrus Gilberti me fecit*. The same signature, the modesty of which was certainly imposed, appears also in other manuscripts, among which is one belonging to the Royal Library in Brussels. The artist who left us his name is not the painter of the miniatures, for we find his signature in manuscripts where the illuminations are definitely ascribed to several different hands and also on pages where there are no miniatures. Nor is he the scribe, nor the copyist. Therefore he could not be one of the main artists of the manuscript, but was simply in charge of its minor decorations.

This Historiated Bible is divided into two volumes, each of which contains about a hundred miniatures. Such an enormous work meant that collaboration among the many technicians had to be organized in every detail. This book, in spite of its length, is written in such a consistent style that one might be led to believe it was copied entirely by the same scribe; this, considering the time it would have taken, is hardly possible. As for the illuminators, to whom the painting of the small pictures was entrusted, they were more free, of course, to follow their own mood. They seem to have made a real effort, though, to harmonize their styles. We are certain that there were two principal contributors to the painting of this book: the manner of one was more linear, the other more pictorial. But it is not always possible to ascribe some of these miniatures to one or the other, because of the impact of that collaboration among the artists on their individual styles. The historian of art, when confined to style as the sole criterion, is indeed confronted with a difficult task.

# The Madonna of the Crescent

PRAYER BOOK OF PHILIP THE BOLD. *Paris. Beginning of the fifteenth century. Additions made in southern Germany for Philip the Good before 1451.*
*164 folios (7 × 10"); 2 historiated initials; 1 medium-sized miniature; 1 full-page miniature.*
*Ms. 11035–37, f. 6 v*

THERE IS NO PROOF whatsoever that the painting that is here illustrated was ever meant to be part of this particular prayer book; rather, it seems to be an addition to the original folios. Moreover, it was made about twenty years after the earliest part of the book and it differs from the frontispiece folios of the *Belles Heures de Jean de Berry* (plates 19 & 20) in that having none of the decorative borders that usually enframe miniatures. Originally it may have been a separate picture painted on vellum and introduced later into the codex. Philip the Bold and the other dukes of Burgundy were, as we shall shortly see, extremely fond of this prayer book. The vicissitudes of this page may well be explained by the changing fortunes of the family.

The theme of the Madonna of the Crescent, symbolizing her holiness, was greatly venerated in the Middle Ages though it cannot be said to have been one of the most popular representations of Christ and His Mother. In spite of its damaged condition, this miniature is perhaps one of the most beautiful figurations of that theme preserved to this day. An additional feature is the crown, which is so much emphasized that the picture might equally well be called the Coronation of the Madonna of the Crescent.

The half-length figure of Mary rests on a narrow crescent. Angels, painted in blue, flutter

around her; they consist of nothing but a head carried on two wings. A large mantle, also blue, wraps the Madonna in its deep and intricate folds. A close look at the fall of the material below the right elbow reveals its resemblance to the rich folds already admired below the Virgin's right knee in the *Belles Heures de Jean de Berry* (plate 20). The drawing is almost identical and the technique exactly the same. In painting the Madonna's face, the artist has been very restrained, using a minimum of means. Just a few strokes of color were sufficient to render the exceptionally delicate features and to give such wonderful depth of expression to the Mother feeding her child. Until the early part of the fifteenth century, no illuminator, nor even painter, had given to the feminine face such classical and human beauty. The child's head is the same as in the Madonna "à la supplique" of the *Belles Heures de Jean de Berry*, especially his manner of turning aside from his mother, probably toward a worshiper. The similarity of the two heads, both painted in the same center, in two exceptionally refined miniatures, is undeniable, but nobody has yet felt entitled to ascribe these two beautiful pictures to the same hand. It may either be that one master has copied the other or that both have copied a third. So much servility on the part of two of the best illuminators working in Paris around 1400 goes against all our traditional ideas on the subject. On the other hand, if one imagines these two figures of a child isolated from their pictorial environment, it would be very difficult to solve the problem of their attribution by their style alone.

The coronation of the Madonna as represented here, is at once simple and dramatic. In spite of its importance, the upper part of the picture does not detract attention from the main subject. (Such a blunder would hardly have been expected in so refined an artist.) He was careful to place the crown according to the inclination of Mary's head, a detail demanding a complicated rendering of perspective; at first glance the result is somewhat surprising.

The six-winged angels supporting the crown were a rediscovery by French painters of this time. They derive from Byzantine art and were brought to France either through Italy or with the Byzantine artists who probably accompanied Emperor Manuel II Palaeologus when he came to stay a year in Paris. We have already met the same type of angels in the Fall of the Angels (plate 21). If we look closer at these angels' faces, we are struck by their resemblance to the very personal style of the Limbourg brothers. One is tempted to conclude that the whole miniature is ascribable to one of them, let us say the eldest, Pol, on account of its perfection. However, when we consider the style of the Madonna's face, where we are struck by the delicacy of her contemplative expression, we must discard the idea, for none of the three brothers has ever attained such facial perfection in any of their known works.

Unfortunately this page has been so damaged that it requires a thorough examination, even a good deal of imagination, to evoke its original splendor. Soon after it was finished, it became an object of intense worship: ex-votos brought from sanctuaries of pilgrimage were glued or sewn around the central picture; these were mostly medals or bits of parchment of all sorts, that were supposed to heal or to protect their owners. Some of them have been preserved and are kept inside the manuscript. The use of a needle on such a delicate page severely damaged and even removed the pigment in several places, and is at least partly responsible for the present condition of the picture. It does not account, though, for the thick layer of black that covers the lower part of the picture and the mantle of the Madonna. This is due to the fact that the owner of the prayer book often worshiped the Madonna like an icon and kissed it devotedly every time he read the prayer on the opposite page. The margins of this folio have become brownish and soiled with fingerprints. The prayer was used to implore assistance against the temptations of the flesh, which explains the presence of the crescent, here meant as a symbol of purity. These blemishes which have partly destroyed one of the most beautiful Madonnas of the Middle Ages are, in another sense, a moving reminder of the devotion of the dukes of Burgundy. The prayer book is made up of some quires written in the time of Philip the Bold; their style reminds us of the technique of the Parisian books around 1380. There are other quires, French also, that date from the time of John the Fearless. The last part was written for Philip the Good by Jean Miélot, in 1451. The manuscript thus passed successively through the hands of the first three dukes of Burgundy, who must have kept it as a work of special value. The prayer book also includes several ex-votos representing St. Veronica holding the veil with the image of the Holy Face. The Veronica, as it was called in the Middle Ages, was supposed to protect one against sudden death. With these ex-votos went a prayer, the text of which has become brown with fingerprints, showing how dear this devotion was to John the Fearless.

For which duke of Burgundy was this Madonna painted? Regardless of whether it is, either directly or indirectly, the work of the Limbourg brothers, it cannot be prior to 1404. The Historiated Bible (Ms. fr. 166 in the Bibliothèque Nationale in Paris), the decoration of which was begun for Philip the Bold and remained unfinished when he died in 1404, is far from attaining the same perfection. The miniature, therefore, dates back to the reign of John the Fearless, though it was not necessarily ordered by him or even included in the manuscript at his personal request. The prayer accompanying the painting was transcribed by Miélot for Philip the Good. It is quite possible that the latter assembled the fragmentary parts of different prayer books belonging to his father and grandfather, and included this picture because it was already an object of veneration in the family. To these remnants, Philip might have added some of his favorite devotions. In any case, this manuscript and the beautiful miniature that goes with it constitute an authentic relic of the dukes of Burgundy.

23

# The Annunciation

BOOK OF HOURS. *Paris. About 1415.*
*247 folios ($8^1/_2 \times 5^3/_4$"); marginal decoration on each page; 22 miniatures.*
*Ms. 10767, f. 30*

THE ANNUNCIATION has always been one of the most popular subjects since the earliest manifestations of art in the Christian world. It has been painted, carved, and engraved more often than many other religious subjects and the best artists in Europe have represented it in unforgettable masterpieces. Popular as this subject may be, the miniature shown here deserves to rank among the best because of its aesthetic merits.

When the angel came to tell Mary of her indispensable role as the Mother of God in the divine drama, she was kneeling at her prie-dieu, reading her book of prayers. Surprised at this unexpected visitation, she just had time to turn around to receive Gabriel's message – thus her gesture with both hands expressing with dignity her deep astonishment. At her side the angel bends on one knee; the salutation he presents to the mother-to-be of Jesus, *Ave gratia plena*, is written on a scroll that gracefully floats in the background. In the top arcade, against a starry sky, God the Father, surrounded by seraphim, participates in the angel's greeting and in Mary's answer. A dove flying down from the Father symbolizes the Holy Ghost.

The scene is complete, bearing the imprint of simplicity and grandeur. Two other interesting details are worth mentioning: a tall lily seems to spring from a vase, which stands on the prie-dieu instead of on the ground, as is usual; the lily stem is long and slender, but there are

Domine labia
mea aperies.
Et os meũ
annunciabit laudem tuã.

a few shorter flowers of various shades drooping over the neck of the vase. This is the only note of fancy to be found in this very classical page. The figures appear against what seems at first to be a gold background. A closer look shows that this is a golden curtain hung on numerous rings along a rail; it replaces the usual colored background.

Every detail contributes toward making this small miniature a perfect picture: the neatness of the drawing, the delicacy of the touch, and the brilliancy of the coloring against a shining gold background. The Paris illuminators had just awakened to the charm of coloring. Until the reign of Charles V, who died in 1380, they contented themselves with blue and red, or with a rather heavy monochrome process. At the end of the century their palette was richer, though it had not yet reached the boldness and the warmth that we find in the angel's mantle, for instance, with its daring shades of red and green, or in his wings which are a real cascade of colors. This harmony is unequaled elsewhere at the beginning of the century, although credit for this enriched coloring should be given to the foreign artists, especially the Italians, who brought it to Paris.

The delicacy of touch mentioned above is noticeable in the accuracy of the patterns on the clothes and in the softness of their folds. It reaches even more striking results in the painting of the human face: to achieve this, the illuminators had needed about twenty years to free themselves from the flat and monotonous drawing we have already noticed in the manuscripts from the Louvre atelier made for Charles V and his court (plates 14 & 16). The linear features were the first to show improvement, but the modeling of the faces and the rendering of the complexion did not appear until the beginning of the next century. Only occasionally, as we have already seen, some pioneer artist shows initiative in this direction. This Paris *Book of Hours* attests that this sensitiveness to the new pictorial values had, at last, become more general.

Critics have ascribed the very personal style of the miniature shown here to the Master of the Hours of the Marshal of Boucicaut, the anonymous author of the Hours painted for that famous French knight. The Marshal of Boucicaut had fought the Turks with John the Fearless, who had been, along with him, one of the few prisoners to escape slaughter. The Master of Boucicaut (as he is generally called) is not merely the author of a few book paintings: he launched a fashion that dominated the entire Parisian production and soon imposed itself on the provincial workshops. The personal style which he had developed became generally adopted within a few years. Although he cannot be compared with the Limbourg brothers or with the Master of Rohan, his style was adopted as law and appears in a considerable number of manuscripts. His manner was, besides, the only one to maintain the line of the Paris tradition, from Jean Pucelle down to the Master of the Breviary of the Duke of Bedford.

The Master of Boucicaut seems to have had a better understanding than any other illuminator of the new trends which found expression in the ateliers of the capital, in an urge for more realism, in a new coloring, and in important innovations in the marginal decoration. These tendencies, as they are used and molded by this great painter, are kept in equilibrium with the taste of the French capital. This was a risky undertaking, bound to deteriorate into mannerism. He was lucky enough to be followed by the Master of Bedford and, perhaps more fortunately still, by that Master's collaborators, who breathed new spirit into French illumination.

We have noticed on the frontispiece folio of the Historiated Bible of Guiard des Moulins (plate 21) that Italian ornamental features had been introduced into French marginal decoration. The presence of the classical Roman acanthus leaf in Italian illumination throughout the Gothic period, and its absence from Paris during about the first two centuries of the new style, are in themselves one of the most significant facts for the study of Western civilization in the Middle Ages. In the border of the miniature described above, this acanthus leaf, endowed with new patterns and new coloring, soon spread through western Europe, while acquiring specific characteristics, individual with each particular workshop. The style of the border is as personal as that of the miniature itself, and the whole page is in the style characteristic of the books of hours of the Master of the Marshal of Boucicaut. The Annunciation page which begins the Hours of Our Lady is usually more decorated than the others and is generally considered the frontispiece page. The other folios containing a miniature show fewer acanthus leaves and those with text only have none of these Italian ornaments. All the pages, however, have marginal decorations.

The coat of arms of the owner has been removed from its shield, but the exceptional quality of the book and the fact that angels are holding the escutcheon lead us to think that these Hours were made perhaps for King Charles VI himself, or for some great prince of his court.

## 24 Two Scenes from the Apocalypse

HISTORIATED BIBLE, *vol. II, in Dutch. Holland. 1431.*
*181 folios (15 1/3 × 11 5/8"); 2 historiated initials; numerous initials; 144 miniatures.*
*Ms. 9020–23, ff. 137 v and 138 v*

THE FIRST MINIATURE in the second volume of this Historiated Bible illustrates several verses from the Apocalypse (8 : 2–6): "And I saw the seven angels which stood before God; and to them were given seven trumpets. And another angel came and stood at the altar, having a golden censer. . . And the seven angels which had the seven trumpets prepared themselves to sound." Then, further on, verse 13: "And I beheld, and heard an angel flying through the midst of heaven, saying with a loud voice, Woe, woe, woe, to the inhabiters of the earth. . .!" As we see, this picture blends together several episodes of chapter 8, for the angel interferes only after the call of the first four trumpets; he comes to tell suffering humanity that the last three calls foretell cataclysms worse than those that have already befallen mankind.

In the second picture are condensed verses from chapter 11: first, "And there was given me a reed like unto a rod: and I was told: Rise, and measure the temple of God, and the altar, and them that worship therein." The rest is inspired by verses 13–16: "And the same hour was there a great earthquake, and the tenth part of the city fell, and in the earthquake were slain of men seven thousand: and the remnant were affrighted, and gave glory to the God of heaven. . . . And the seventh angel sounded; and there were great voices in heaven, saying, The kingdoms of this world are become the kingdoms of our Lord, and of his Christ; and he shall reign forever

and ever. And the four and twenty elders, which sat before God on their seats, fell upon their faces, and worshipped God. . . . "

The seventh angel is the last of the group represented in the first miniature. He is completing the purification of the world, thus preparing the advent of the Lord. However, these two pictures do not follow one directly after the other: the illuminator has painted two others which concern the two intermediate chapters.

The artist has certainly done his best to introduce into these miniatures all that could possibly be elicited from the sacred text: the presence of the eagle, for instance, in the first picture, that of the angel carrying a rod, and also the figure of the Lord, in the second. This may confuse the modern reader who is unaware of this practice common to all illustrators of the Middle Ages, as he may well lose track of the chronological significance of the events. Indeed, a text providing so many actors is, in terms of composition, very tempting for a decorator. In this respect some of our miniatures are masterpieces; The Four and Twenty Elders Worshipping God is the best example of this on these pages.

These two miniatures were chosen above all for their colors. Nowhere else can we find such extraordinary shades as this olive green and mauve, and nowhere are they used with such skill and imagination. The violent colors of the angels' robes and the contrasts among the Elders' mantles are unique, so far, in the history of medieval miniatures. The results are not always pleasing but the artist does catch our eye with his startling colors; moreover, the type of face he adopts for his characters – their unreal greenish complexions and their overemphasized pupils – would not be out of place in many modern paintings. Thus, in spite of their mistakes, the innovators of this craft paved the way for the more conventional masters who benefited from their experiments.

We regret being limited to these two miniatures for our appreciation of the vast and varied iconography displayed in this Historiated Bible. For the execution of a work of this importance, containing more than two hundred pictures, a large number of miniaturists must have been employed. Since each of them was allowed to paint in his own manner, the individual artists are easy to distinguish. In most manuscripts decorated in other countries, the different hands, though discernible, usually strive for a certain harmony with a view to preserving the uniformity of the whole. But in Dutch books we may see a master of the art of landscape followed by an illuminator who prefers brilliant gold backgrounds, or an artisan with hard outline drawing who uses his colors like an enameler, working next to a true painter who relies entirely on the elaborate effects of his subtle mixture of colors. Such freedom may be accounted for by the absence of a rich, exacting patronage, with the result that, within a few decades, several styles of manuscripts developed that existed nowhere else.

Dutch illumination is also orginal in its iconographical innovations. The books decorated by these miniaturists are mostly religious texts, books for liturgical or pious use. The artist whose task it was to illustrate them had, therefore, centuries of varying traditions behind him, which might well have exhausted the subject matter. This was not so, however; these masters have proved to be real inventors in a domain admittedly popularized. The Bible of course afforded them an immense field of opportunity where they could give their imagination full rein, especially in the Apocalypse, where one senses at once the immense richness of the symbolism.

This copy of the Bible was written in 1431, not for a religious house but for a layman, a certain Claes Petersoen, a fact peculiar in itself. In the middle of the fifteenth century, Holland was the only center in which such long texts were still transcribed, and also decorated with numerous miniatures. Let us notice that this Historiated Bible translated into Dutch corresponds to those historiated Bibles in French of about 1300. Nevertheless, the reason for the marked interest aroused in the Bible in Holland is a different one. There was at that time a very lively religious feeling that expressed its beliefs and even its theological concepts in sincere and simple language. The movement, called *devotio moderna*, came to penetrate even the lay public of Holland. The result was a great number of books of hours and even Bibles written in the vulgar tongue and, of course, many works more directly concerned with the ascetic life. This more individual piety prepared the ground, historically, for Protestantism which later asserted the same needs.

If we compare plates 16, 21, 22, and 23 to plate 15 and to this one, we realize that there is a world of difference between the French and the Dutch manners. The former reveal a tradition that constantly strives to remain elegant and well balanced while progressively assimilating the discoveries of the native illuminators and of their foreign collaborators; the latter, on the contrary, affirms from the beginning its love for realism which enriches itself at an ever-increasing pace, and gives free rein, for better and for worse, to all its creative fantasies.

A note written in red has been added by the copyist to one of the flyleaves at the end of the first volume of this manuscript. It tells us that the Bible belonged to Nicolas, son of Peter (Claes Petersoen), and that it was written in 1431. The Bible was therefore made for its first owner. Another note concerns the copyist Claes Brouwer and keeps us informed of the progress of the work, though there are more miniatures than the total number he mentions. The accounts were probably settled before the Bible was completed, or perhaps the text was originally divided into three parts, or volumes, instead of the two we have preserved. It has unfortunately not yet been possible to locate with more precision the origin of this very important work.

## 25 The Entombment

BOOK OF HOURS, *in Latin and Dutch. Delft. About 1440.*
*151 folios ($6^1/_8 \times 4^1/_8$"); 22 miniatures in grisaille.*
*Ms. 21696, f. 50 v*

IT WAS CERTAINLY daring for a medieval painter, accustomed by tradition to dread empty spaces, to compose his picture on a diagonal. This meant leaving a whole corner empty while squeezing the figures into what remained hardly half of the painting. The format of the miniature really necessitated some such composition for it would have been impossible to arrange the figures in the width without reducing their size as well as that of the tomb. The artist was rewarded in that the originality of his composition unfailingly attracts attention and gives more life to the picture, for he could thus paint the faces in more detail.

The tomb into which the body of Christ is lowered by Joseph of Arimathea and Nicodemus is in the center of the picture. The body has a somewhat unearthly grace in spite of the traces of blood near the wounds. The limp trunk, the neck, and the curved arms do not convey the impression that they are rigid in death. Also, Christ is not wrapped in a shroud; He is clad in a large mantle, fastened in the front with a brooch, that partly hides His body. The face is a little crooked, as if the artist had tried to express grief; the mouth seems to be distorted and the eyes slightly oblique. The representation of Christ is inferior to that of Joseph of Arimathea and Nicodemus. The latter, who stands near Christ's feet, seems particularly lifelike as he lifts the body below the knees; the tucked-up sleeve and the arm half-hidden by Christ's mantle

are well-observed and finely rendered details. The Pharisee's profile is carefully drawn and perhaps intentionally emphasized; its roughness contrasts with the aristocratic features and expression of the man who supports the upper part of the body at the other side of the tomb. The movement of this man's arms is correct but the gesture of his hands is weak and inadequate.

The group including St. John and the pious women is somewhat less successful. The faces are more uniform and of the type we find in most of the miniatures ascribed to this same hand: the pupils are too strongly emphasized and the lower jaws are angular. The attitudes of the women are all alike except for Mary, who is stooping with an infinite tenderness to kiss her Son's hand. This movement enables the painter to disclose the faces of the figures standing in the rear, particularly St. John, who otherwise would be entirely hidden. Mary Magdalen is recognizable in the group by her headdress, which is much more elegant than the other women's simple veils, and also by the privileged place she holds near the tomb, next to Christ. The scene is so vivid that one is under the impression of being present and marvels at the painter's skill in conveying this feeling in such a small surface. This he does by means of the simplest pictorial process: grisaille, touched up with a little gold on the sleeves and on the ornaments of the clothing. He is indeed an absolute master in the use of silverpoint, which has given the picture such depth, and a velvety soft modeling that the years do not seem to have altered.

The miniature is surrounded by a frame, increasing the effect of a real picture; this illusion is further enhanced by the absence of marginal decoration. The idea of the drawn-in frame had been in favor at the end of the Romanesque period and we find it again in a few isolated manuscripts at the end of the fourteenth and the beginning of the fifteenth century; it was also used in Bohemia and in Italy, but always accompanied by other decorations. In this book we have authentic pictures physically unconnected with the text. The miniature reproduced in plate 25 and all the others in the manuscript are painted on intercalated folios, the recto of which is always a blank page. This characteristic became at that time a monopoly of Dutch religious imagery. The commerce in pictures made in Utrecht was so popular that in 1427 it was forbidden to sell them in Bruges!

In most Dutch manuscripts, the Hours of Our Lady are illuminated with eight miniatures relating to the Passion cycle, while in France and in the southern Netherlands, the cycle of the Nativity was generally preferred. The distinction is not quite exact, however, for we sometimes find large miniatures representing scenes from the Passion, followed by illuminated initials devoted to the childhood of Christ, or the same subjects in a reversed order. The placing of such representations is important in that it may be due to the advent of some foreign artist, thus accounting for stylistic changes that would otherwise remain unexplained.

From the calendar it appears that this Book of Hours was intended for the bishopric of Utrecht.

We also learn from a short sentence written on one of the simplest of the marginal decorations that the manuscript was copied and illuminated in the convent of Val Josaphat in Delft. Like most of the Dutch books of hours, especially those executed by the Regular Canons, this one shows their authentic mastery of the art of calligraphy; all the minor decorations, such as the initials and the borders, are done with the utmost care and should probably be ascribed to the Augustine Canonesses. They may also have painted the miniatures, though this is by no means proven. We are once more confronted with the problem that concerns the painting of images by lay artists, which can only be elucidated by a complete study of the manuscripts belonging to the category represented here.

All the books of hours decorated in this style, most of them dated around 1440, have one quality in common: their sensitiveness to human values. The result is a craving for more veracity, the desire to be free of mannerism, the pleasure of painting figures as one sees them. It is in the modeling of their faces that this quality reaches its culmination. We must remember that it found its first expression in Dutch illumination (plate 15: Gelre's *Armorial*). We shall see further on that it will continue to enrich itself and that in this respect no other school can be compared with it.

## 26 St. Augustine Reading His *City of God*

ST. AUGUSTINE, The City of God, *first part of the translation by Raoul de Presles. Southern Netherlands. 1445.*
*449 folios ($16^1/_2 \times 11^1/_4$"); 1 large frontispiece miniature with a marginal border; 10 small miniatures.*
*Ms. 9015, f. 1*

ONE IS STRUCK, at the very first glance, by the composite character of this miniature. The format of the scene is not comprehensible at once. We will immediately see the town outlined on the right side of the background, but we fail to understand the presence of the king in the foreground, standing beside a group of rocks. The oddness of the presentation is, fortunately, counterbalanced by the high quality of the picture. But its style poses one of the most complex problems in the history of Netherlandish illumination.

The picture is divided into four parts: St. Augustine and his audience, King Clovis, the City of God, and the landscape in the center. We shall see in a moment why this landscape must be considered an important part of the whole and not just a means of filling unwanted space. To avoid any misunderstanding, the name of St. Augustine has been written on the back of the lectern. He is seated on an episcopal throne, wearing his miter and reading the book of which he is the author to a select and apparently very interested audience. An angel flies down from the skies to bring him divine inspiration while an eagle, symbolizing the profundity of thought of this Father of the Church, stares at the dazzling sun of Theology.

The attitudes of the figures seated at the saint's feet are varied and their faces individualized: they deserve a special study. The audience itself is divided into three groups. In the first, the

more numerous one, the figures are seated on a bench at the right of the baldachin; some of them have such marked personalities that it is clear they are portraits. The tallest, whose sharp profile is framed by an ermine-bordered hood, could be John of Bavaria, count of Holland. Other identical faces and even attitudes have been found in a miniature of the *Hours of Turin* (burned in 1904), in which a count of Holland is represented landing on a beach. All these characters of high rank are either discussing the newly presented book or sunk in deep thought. At the foot of the dais, a little to the left, sits a Benedictine monk in a professor's chair, turning his back to the holy bishop. This detail, as well as the fact that he holds his book erect, suggests that he is taking part in the master's teaching and thus may be Raoul de Presles, the translator, thanks to whom St. Augustine's writings were known in French. Facing the author and the translator are two listeners in plain clothing, probably representing the common audience. Raoul de Presles had translated the *City of God* at the request of Charles V; this is why the King of France is often represented on the frontispiece folio of the copies. In the Brussels manuscript, however, and in several others executed in the Netherlands, the royal personage is no longer Charles V, but Clovis, whose name we read on the left sleeve of the royal mantle.

In the prologue of his work, Raoul de Presles tells the story of Clovis which has apparently inspired the illuminator. The banner, the chrism for the royal anointing carried in a flask by the dove, and the blazon of France presented by an angel, certainly all concern either king, Charles V or Clovis. The rocks on the right may be symbolical, and they serve the purpose of counterbalancing the rather crowded left half of the miniature. These rocks also appear in several miniatures belonging to the *Hours of Turin* quoted above. The royal ensign has been painted out of proportion, for the purpose of separating the parts of the miniature.

The town in the background is, of course, the "City of God." There are very few instances in medieval manuscripts of a town painted with such meticulous care and so much accuracy in the details. The Gothic church, almost symmetrical with its tower and transept in the middle, is the most striking feature of this accumulation of roofs and façades. We find this entire city again, painted as it is here, in the background of Jan van Eyck's *Virgin and Child with Saints and a Donor* in the Frick Collection in New York; once more we are confronted with the "Eyckian" tradition. We should like to identify this very unusual church: the original St. Paul's Cathedral in London has been named as a model, and there is undeniably some ground for this suggestion. One would prefer, however, to proceed by elimination and to ascertain first that no other church existed in western Europe having a nave as long as the choir.

It may seem strange that the landscape between St. Augustine's throne and the heavenly city should be considered only the fourth important feature of the picture. Beautiful as it may be, with its hills and trees, its rows of bushes and its horizon of snow-capped mountains, has it any other purpose than to function as a link among the main subjects of the painting? Strangely enough, this landscape is identical, detail for detail, to that seen in the background of the *Adoration of the Lamb by the Virgins* in the *Hours of Turin.* One finds there the same type of trees with their individualized leaves. This resemblance is hard to account for if the two pictures have not been painted by the same hand. What could be the reason for copying a landscape, not particularly interesting in itself, since it is only a minor feature in the miniature? The comparison of the two manuscripts brings an important contribution to the question of whether one should ascribe the miniature in the *Hours of Turin* to Jan van Eyck.

In spite of having features in common with other works, this miniature is much in advance of the general production around 1440. Several decades will elapse before one comes across any comparable work in Flemish illumination. The silhouette of the town is unique, even in these centers, until the end of the reign of Philip the Good in 1467. The figures are those of real human beings; their gestures, expressive as well as varied, have no counterpart, even in works of high quality. We should also draw attention to the beauty of the color, while we regret the tendency to be content with somewhat dark shades. As for the composition, it is excellent, and not impaired by the difficult task of including three subjects in the same painting.

The miniature just described belongs to a monumental page where angels and humans, including two horsemen in the purest Eyckian style, are painted among the red, blue, and gold of flowers and acanthus leaves. An escutcheon held by two standing angels adorns the initial and bears the coat of arms of Jean Chevrot, bishop of Tournai, who ordered this copy of the *City of God.* A Dominican monk, Nicolas Cotin, tells us in the colophon that he finished the transcription in 1445. As a manuscript was never decorated with pictures until the text was completed, the illumination is therefore later than this date. The miniature, however, was made very soon after the transcription, for its marginal ornaments are more in the Boucicaut tradition than in the style of the margins during the Burgundian period proper, which starts a little before 1450.

We have no other elements with which to identify the artist's hand; the picture is certainly not by Jan van Eyck, but it is unquestionably "Eyckian." We know, besides, that there is no relation between the very personal style of Jan van Eyck and the rest of the Flemish miniaturists. Should we therefore turn our thoughts to some Dutch painter, traveling southward to practice his art because Philip the Good had just then suppressed the local princely patronage by taking possession of the county of Holland, the duchy of Gelder and the bishopric of Utrecht? It is a tempting suggestion indeed, for it is only in these areas that the "Eyckian" tradition flourished. Such manuscripts are the most precious documents for the historian of illumination: they urge one to reconsider the classifications too easily accepted before.

# 27 Simon Nockart Presenting the *Chroniques de Hainaut* to Philip the Good

JACQUES DE GUISE, Chroniques de Hainaut, *translated by Jean Wauquelin, Vol. I. Mons. 1448.*
*449 folios (16 3/4 × 11 1/4"); 40 miniatures with marginal borders.*
*Ms. 9242, f. 1*

THIS FRONTISPIECE folio of the *Chroniques de Hainaut* is certainly the most famous miniature in the collection of manuscripts belonging to the Royal Library in Brussels. This manifestation of princely patronage is an extraordinary record of the great Duke of Burgundy's personal distinction as well as a testimony of his political power and wealth. The picture goes far beyond a mere interest in local history: it displays all the features with which our imagination is accustomed to adorn the Middle Ages; from this point of view it deserves to be considered a classic.

Before pointing out its aesthetic merits, we should mention the circumstances in which the copy of the *Chroniques de Hainaut* was presented to Philip the Good; also, we should try to identify as far as possible his principal attendants. We need not linger over the figure of the Duke of Burgundy himself, with his noble bearing, standing apart with his son at his side. The councilors grouped on his right deserve closer attention, for they were the true artisans of the greatness of the Burgundian States and two of them, at least, are known to us. First, Chancellor Rolin whose face bears the strain of heavy responsibilities, which probably accounts for the absorbed look in his eyes and for his complete unconcern with what is going on. A little further from the duke, but more in the foreground and obviously participating in the ceremony, stands Jean Chevrot, the owner of the beautiful copy of the *City of God* (plate 26). Chevrot was

not only one of the duke's main councilors, but he was also, as bishop of Tournai, the only ecclesiastical dignitary in the newly founded States of Burgundy. These two great dignitaries of the new court are represented here with complete fidelity as we see by comparing them with their portraits in the pictures painted by Jan van Eyck and Rogier van der Weyden. (The third personage, unfortunately unidentified, appears again in the frontispiece folio of the *Girart de Roussillon*, a manuscript belonging to the National Library in Vienna.) The group on the right side of the picture shows the eight principal members of the aristocracy of the Burgundian court, all Knights of the Golden Fleece. The elegance of their garments reveals the spirit developing among these noblemen, their fate so altered by their master's startling rise to power. I suggest two identifications. The tall Knight of the Golden Fleece, dressed in black and standing not far from Charles the Bold, is Philip's eldest natural son, Anthony, called *le Grand Bâtard de Bourgogne*, who spent all his life fighting his father's wars. The second character, on the far right in the foreground, is Jean de Croy, and the kneeling figure who is presenting the duke with the Chronicles is Simon Nockart. These identifications are based on the following historical facts connected with the milieu from which this manuscript issued.

In the literary movement that developed in consequence of the duke of Burgundy's political achievements, Jean Wauquelin, who was established in Mons between 1440 and 1452, must be considered the first author of importance. He is also the first publisher – in the modern sense of the word – of the luxury manuscripts executed for the new patron in a new style. We find three texts among his productions, written in 1448; in all three of them the deliberate flattery of the new sovereign is evident. Each volume has a miniature of exceptional richness on the frontispiece page, all three having several elements in common in their presentation of the book to the duke. These manuscripts are, namely: *L'histoire d'Alexandre* (Ms. fr. 9342, Paris, Bibliothèque Nationale), *Girart de Roussillon* (Ms. 2549, Vienna, National Library) and this *Chroniques de Hainaut*. Alexander was the pre-eminent model for the medieval conquerors. Girart de Roussillon was, according to legend, the first Duke of Burgundy and was said to have defeated Charles the Bold, king of France, on twenty occasions. The flattery is too obvious to require attention. As for the county of Hainaut, its history was so illustrious that the new count, Philip the Good himself, could be proud of continuing the traditions of his predecessors. As we can see, the author-publisher wanted above all to please. Elsewhere we learn from Wauquelin, in another of his prologues, that his patron is Jean de Croy and that he received payments from this nobleman. On the other hand, in the preface of the *Chroniques de Hainaut* we read that Simon Nockart, another of the duke's councilors from Hainaut, is the promoter of this translation in three big volumes. In the frontispieces of both the *Girart* and the *Alexandre*, the duke receives the manuscript from the same personage, whose plain face and pug nose are so individual that this is undisputably a portrait. And who could it portray, if not Wauquelin? Why then do we not find him also in the *Chroniques*? Here, the donor, with his aquiline nose and aristocratic features, bears no resemblance to the donor in the two other portraits: he is an entirely different person. Since it was at Simon Nockart's personal request that Wauquelin translated the work of Jacques de Guise, it was naturally the privilege of Simon Nockart to present the copy. If he is indeed the donor in the Brussels manuscript, then the nobleman in the green tunic behind him ought to be Jean de Croy: he is stepping out of the group to give the donor a sign of his protection or, perhaps, to take part in the presentation. Besides, he is to be found in the two other frontispieces painted exactly as he is here, in profile. In the *Girart* he is laying his hand on Wauquelin's shoulder, thus attesting his patronage. Incidentally, it is only fair to say that these two other frontispieces, especially that in the *Girart de Roussillon*, are superior when compared to other contemporary presentation miniatures. We have thus in this picture an authentic suite of portraits, the first of importance in the history of book painting. It is probably for that reason that the setting in the frontispiece was not given much attention, though its perspective is faultless and the details are scrupulously reproduced. The most exquisite taste has presided over the distribution of light and shade. The palette, moreover, is about the richest conceivable. For these reasons combined, this miniature is one of the most perfect specimens of the art of the Middle Ages to have been preserved. The years unfortunately have caused it some damage: the pigment is peeling in several places, making some parts of the faces look shapeless.

The picture has been ascribed to Rogier van der Weyden; more recently, he was alleged to be the author of the drawing only; there is no proof, however, that this miniature was not the work of an illuminator. The drawing of this presentation scene was reproduced four years later, detail for detail, in another manuscript: *Le Gouvernement des Princes* (Ms. 9043, Brussels, Royal Library) but with an entirely different coloring; this makes us think that a sketch of this subject was kept in Mons, in the workshop from which the *Chroniques de Hainaut* was issued and where the *Gouvernement des Princes* was also executed four years later. Could not this account for the close relationship existing between our frontispiece and those of the Vienna *Girart de Roussillon* and the Paris *Alexandre*? Such a miniature, if made by a painter, could be executed only after all other work on the book had been completed in the workshop; passing then from the painter's studio directly into the duke's library, the manuscript could not have been given back to the illuminators for the purpose of copying the frontispiece. Anyhow, the question of the authorship of the picture should not prevail over our appreciation of its intrinsic value; whoever its author may be, the frontispiece miniature of the *Chroniques de Hainaut* remains one of the true masterpieces of Flemish painting.

28

# The Patriarch of India Approaching the Tomb of the Apostle Thomas

DÉBAT SUR L'HONNEUR *and other works on morality, translated by Jean Miélot. Brussels. 1449–50.*
*48 folios (16 × 11¼"); 8 large miniatures.*
*Ms. 9278–80, f. 45*

THE TITLE OF this manuscript can lead to some confusion, for the book comprises three different texts, all three translated by Jean Miélot: *Un débat entre trois chevaleureux princes* (Alexander, Hannibal, and Scipio) and *La Controversie de Noblesse* (ascribed to Bonus Accursius), and an anonymous work called *Rapport sur les faits et miracles de Monseigneur Saint Thomas l'Apôtre*. The miniature reproduced here is an illustration from the latter work.

The subject of the picture is explained in the text itself, in which we read that every year, on the feast day of the Apostle Thomas, the Patriarch of India used to go to the saint's tomb. The crowd of people following the prelate or coming to meet him are entreating him to give them a share of the balm which burns, without ever being consumed, in a golden lamp in front of the saint's shrine. The procession is walking from the walls of the town under the guidance of the prelate who rides a mule. They are approaching the sanctuary on a small hill, painted in the center of the picture. Newcomers are joining the group at the foot of the hill to add their voices to the general hue and cry.

The subject is of particular interest since it does not pertain to a mere legend but to an old tradition in the Church. This tradition may not refer properly to St. Thomas himself, but it is otherwise accurate: when the twelve Apostles dispersed to preach the Gospel to the world, the

Apostle Thomas, who was more adventurous than the others, is said to have gone to India and settled there. As a matter of fact, a Christian sect was eventually implanted on the subcontinent; but this probably happened at a later date than that propounded by the tradition. This sect lived in a group and was soon cut off from the Church, which had meanwhile become established in Rome. When the Portuguese landed in India, they encountered this Christian population, found them guilty of ignoring the proper rites and doctrine, and put them to death.

After the fierce resistance to the Turks by the Byzantine emperor had given the alarm to the Western countries, their consciousness of the Turkish menace was awakened. The Occident began to take a deep interest in Asia, the Near East, and even the Far East. Traveling was much more common in those days than we sometimes imagine, but, unfortunately, very few of these adventurers and pioneers were able to keep a written record of their experiences. We read, for instance, in the *Chroniques de Jean de Wavrin* about the exploits of Geoffroy de Thoisy, who sailed with the knights *de la langue de Bourgogne* from Rhodes to Constantinople and on to the Black Sea. We shall soon be given further proof of this growing concern for the East (plate 32), which increased greatly after the fall of Constantinople in 1453.

The illuminator has made an effort to endow the painting with a somewhat Oriental touch: we notice that some of his personages wear the tarboosh, others the turban; there is also a bulbous tower above the roofs; for the rest, however, the painter contents himself with the clothing and the buildings of Western countries.

The pictorial technique of this painting is most unusual. The tints are so thin and delicate that they look at first sight like watercolor. However, we soon discover that some details, the trees and mantles, for instance, are painted in gouache of the normal thickness, which elsewhere has been diluted. We wonder why other artists never thought of using this process, for it produces astonishing effects in the modeling and a liveliness that well suits the anecdotic style of this type of miniature. We have already pointed out the increasing interest in books in the newly founded States of Burgundy; it aroused literary talents that resulted in the creation of new texts, a fair number of which were concerned with historical events (*Chroniques de Hainaut*, plate 27). Differing from the Bibles and other liturgical books with which the Dutch illuminators had to be satisfied, these texts opened wide horizons to the painters entrusted with their illumination. The main purpose of this new kind of illustration was evidently to bring into the picture something of the liveliness of the narration, and here the miniaturist has fully succeeded. The variety in the grouping of the garments and in the attitudes gives us the impression that we are taking part in the procession. This painter cannot compare, however, with the Master of the *Chroniques de Hainaut* (plate 27) in his management of the space left at his disposal. The foreground is convincing and the town in the background with its shadows so skillfully emphasized, but the open space between is the weak area of the picture. Only a great master could have overcome this difficulty. The details of the landscape, such as the large rock in the middle ground or the green trees in front of the tower, are out of proportion. We cannot help feeling, though, that this clumsiness, even artlessness, provide part of the charm of the medieval miniatures; this is best demonstrated in the winding paths running across the picture, which are intended to convey the illusion of depth.

Critics have ascribed this page to Jean Le Tavernier. Its style is indeed very close to that of the latter's typical grisailles. The transcription of the *Débat sur l'honneur* was made by Jean Miélot in 1449–50 in Brussels, and the miniatures are thus contemporary. Le Tavernier's work allegedly preserved in this book would therefore be a little earlier than his grisailles made for the Book of Hours of Philip the Good (Ms. 76. f. 2, The Hague, Royal Library), for which he was paid in 1454. This would account for dissimilarities in the two techniques, including his way of painting trees. Our picture would be a work of his earlier period, already characterized by the thin, strongly marked noses of the figures. The verve noticed here will develop in the *Conquêtes de Charlemagne* (plate 36). The outlined towns also frequently appear in the latter manuscript, in which our illuminator reaches the maturity of his art. Do we only have in the *Débat sur l'honneur* a preliminary stage, less characterized than the subsequent works? Later on the progress in technique will accentuate the artist's vigor, perhaps at the expense of the spontaneity we admire in this earlier work.

## 29 The Tree of Jesse

BREVIARY OF PHILIP THE GOOD. *Flanders. About 1455–59.*
*528 folios ($11^5/_8 \times 3^3/_8$"); 6 large miniatures; 14 small miniatures; 7 historiated initials; numerous marginal decorations.*
*Ms. 9511, f. 15*

AROUND 1450, large manuscripts became fashionable, and the publishers kept in line with the contemporary taste of the connoisseurs. The size of these volumes usually makes it difficult to give a reproduction of any page in full and thus to convey an adequate idea of the typical production of this period. This opportunity is therefore all the more welcome, to reproduce in full size a page chosen from a book comparatively small for the epoch. Indeed, when one must ascertain the date and especially the origin of a manuscript, it is often more important to consider the style of the whole page, such as it appears – the text, the writing, the initials, the line endings, and the borders – than to rely only on the miniature proper. The miniature painters were not, like the other technicians of the manuscripts, attached to a particular center: they traveled from one place to another, and thus cannot provide us with any criterion stable enough to trace the origin and the history of painting.

The decorative frame of the miniature represented here is exceptionally simple for a mid-fifteenth-century manuscript. All preserved examples show the more or less lavish use of acanthus foliage; in Chevrot's *City of God*, for instance, it is almost the sole ornament. Here, the illuminator seems to have avoided acanthus leaves lest he should overcrowd the frame, since an overdecorated margin would distract attention from the miniature in the center. Moreover,

Sabbato in adventu do-
mini ad vesperas super
psalmos. antiphona Be-
nedictus. psalmus. Ipm.
Cum ceteris antiphonis
et psalmis. Infra. Caplm.

Ecce
dies
veni-
unt
dicit
dns
et suscitabo david germe

we are told that the Breviary of Philip the Good was made after an older Paris copy, which was in the duke's possession and probably dated back to the time when the usual marginal decoration was limited to vine foliage interspersed with small flowers. The similarity of style between the new Breviary and its supposed model should not, however, lead us to believe it was executed in Paris, for the vine leaves assume the rough lancet-shaped pattern which is a degenerate form of the cinquefoil used in the heyday of the French manuscript. Nevertheless, the decoration as well as all the other techniques of the book are ascribable to a master of his craft. A master was also the scribe who wrote the faultless Gothic script we admire in the reproduction, and maintained this level of perfection over the two thousand pages of the manuscript, from the first folio to the very last.

The large initial on this page has been set in a quite uncommon place. Normally, in a well-balanced page the letter should stand in the left column, but the rubric here was too long. We know of no other case of this kind. Here, the initial is very bulky and contrasts with the sobriety of the frame.

The miniature displays such a freshness of color and light and its gold is so brilliant that this small defect does not impair its splendor. The gold background is an archaism; but could the illuminator have chosen any better way to give relief to the very disconnected subject of this picture? The use of any color would have subdued the symphony of light displayed here; it would have prevented its repetition in the rest of the painting and limited the varied use of its components. If, for instance, the painter had adopted the customary sky background, he would have had to renounce all the varieties of blue which is his favorite color and which he uses so skillfully; he could not have applied the rich green that he chose for the tree and the corollas.

The Tree of Jesse is a well-known theme, inspired from Isaiah. Jesse was the father of David, from whom Christ is the direct descendant. The twelve crowned figures represent the twelve kings of Judah, the tribe to which the Messiah belongs. At the top of the miniature, in a starry sky, God the Father surrounded by angels is giving His blessing to the Mother and Child below him. In His left hand He holds the globe and also a cruciform banner which is usually the emblem of Christ triumphant after the Resurrection. It may have been added as a sign of the glorious mission that would one day be the Child's. Jesse lies in a flowery meadow, protected by the walls of a terrace; his head is resting on a huge, somewhat incongruous cushion. The tree's graceful scroll of foliage bears flowers with wide-open corollas supporting the Virgin and the kings of Judah. There is great diversity in the coloring. Also the attitudes of the kings, whose faces are very individualized, are varied, and each of them plays a different instrument.

The iconography of the Tree of Jesse is very old; it came back into fashion in the middle of the fifteenth century, especially in the northern Netherlands. Incidental details vary from one picture to another. What characterizes the miniature represented here is the importance given to the figure of Jesse as compared with the small and modest Virgin. The Dutch manuscripts show several examples of the kings of Judah seated in corollas (Hours of Mary van Vronensteyn, plate 37), but nowhere do they play music. These royal musicians are probably not original with our painter but they contribute to the picture a liveliness we find in no other contemporary "Tree of Jesse."

In the two-volume Breviary of Philip the Good there is one other miniature by the same hand that painted the Tree of Jesse; it is a very original Nativity that has become popular since being reproduced in color. These two illustrations are in the first, or Winter, part of the book. All others, whether large or small, and even the historiated initials, are in the well-known manner of William Vrelant. Since this second artist is in no way comparable to the master shown here, we wonder why the latter's contribution was limited to the first two miniatures. Here are two possible answers: either the artist canceled the contract, which seems rather reckless on the part of an illuminator working for the duke, or he died shortly after he had started his work. In all the illuminated books from the period of Philip the Good, no colored miniature in the same manner has yet been discovered.

Nevertheless, the two miniatures have more than once been ascribed to Jean Le Tavernier, the talented master of the grisailles in Aubert's *Chroniques et Conquêtes de Charlemagne* (plate 36). Archive documents attest that this Audenarde illuminator also painted in colors, and on this ground, he has been credited with several book paintings, such as those which illustrate the *Débat sur l'honneur*. Our two miniatures differ from these both in style and in technique. One never finds in Le Tavernier's miniatures the fleshy flat-nosed faces that we see on some of the kings of Judah; on the other hand, most of the latter's faces have a pleasant, human look and do not remind us at all of those of the Master of Audenarde, who has a preference for bony features with a long nose and pointed chin. The hands, however, are perhaps more in his manner. We should remember that a new style was evolving at that time, bringing together the most diversified talents; these tended to copy each other, sometimes unconsciously, sometimes deliberately. We do not know to what extent a master could impose his own style on his collaborators, especially if they were more gifted than himself! Whatever the answer to this may be, the Tree of Jesse will remain a very original work of Flemish illumination. As for the pages which are credited to William Vrelant, they may be a little after 1455 for he was using this particular style in Bruges at about this time. Since the two techniques succeed each other in this Breviary without interacting, the rest of the decoration must have been made not much later than that date.

30

# René d'Anjou Watching the Mortification of Vain Pleasure

RENÉ D'ANJOU, Le Mortifiement de Vaine Plaisance. *Perhaps southern Netherlands. Sometime after 1455.*
*210 folios (11 × 7⅞"); 9 miniatures; 2 marginal decorations.*
*Ms. 10308, f. 76*

ALL THE PREFERENCE in the Middle Ages for a very elaborate and rather prim symbolism is manifest in this very decorative page. Its true significance would remain extremely mysterious were the theme not explained. A brief summary of this work by René d'Anjou, king of Sicily and Jerusalem, will provide the indispensable data for full comprehension of this picture.

The pious Soul is disconsolate; its Heart, called Vain Pleasure (*Vaine Plaisance*), keeps diverting it from its course toward God. Because of Vain Pleasure the Soul has failed and dares not appear in front of Sovereign Justice. Two ladies offer their help, Fear of God (*Crainte de Dieu*) and Perfect Contrition (*Parfaite Contrition*), who both encourage it to rid itself of the slavery imposed by Vain Pleasure. Convinced of the necessity of humiliating its Heart by the practice of a mortifying asceticism, the Soul hands over Vain Pleasure to them. Fear of God and Perfect Contrition take away their precious burden into a wonderful garden placed on a hill. In this paradise are four ladies: Sovereign Love (*Souverain Amour*), True Hope (*Vraie Espérance*), Firm Faith (*Ferme Foy*), and Divine Grace (*Grace Divine*). The two visitors tell them all about the torments inflicted by the Heart on the pious Soul. Firm Faith agrees to nail the Heart on the Cross to purify it by making it participate in Christ's Passion. One after the other the four ladies pierce Vain Pleasure and hand it over, gentle and humbled, to Fear of God and Perfect

Coment les iiii. dames tiennent le cuer de lame sur une croix.

Lors les deux dames depuis quilz furent sur le fust de la croix mirent le cuer a lendroit proprement que le tresbenoit et precieux

Contrition, who bring back the crucified Heart to the pious Soul. The latter is frightened at first for it is unable to recognize this Heart it had known to be so "treacherous and spiteful" (*félon et si despiteux*); it then thanks the ladies and praises God Almighty in its prayers.

This miniature is the seventh illustration of the text it decorates. It describes the crucifixion of Vain Pleasure. Fear of God is standing under a huge sword and Perfect Contrition is holding a bundle of rods; they have just arrived in the paradisiac garden and have entrusted their burden to the four ladies who are slightly apart on the left. Faith and Hope are already thrusting the nails into the Heart: one is driving in a steel nail and the other a silver nail, Charity is about to add a golden one. Each nail releases a definite number of drops of blood, each drop symbolizing one of Vain Pleasure's attachments to the things of this world, from which it is thus liberated. Here, the illuminator has made a slight mistake, for the gold nail is represented as already stuck in the Heart whereas, in the text, this golden nail is the last to be driven in. In turn comes Divine Grace, bearing a crown which is more resplendent than the sun; she is preparing herself to pierce the already bruised Heart. All that is left of Vain Pleasure is supposed to be drained by this last wound. The author, King René, who has been following Fear of God and Perfect Contrition, stops at the garden gate to witness the mortification. On the front of the door and on the upright of the cross the illuminator has written a text, the meaning of which is impossible to understand though the letters are perfectly legible. It must be one of the many cryptograms encountered so often in medieval manuscripts, to which the key has not yet been found.

The very condensed composition of this complex subject reminds us of the technique commonly used in tapestry. The different figures are arranged in tiers as if the spectator were enjoying an elevated view of the whole scene. The sky is here reduced to a narrow strip near the top of the picture. The adoption of such a point of view brings necessary changes, and limits the possibilities of rendering space. In spite of the disproportion between the figures and the trees, the clumsiness of the movements and the coarseness of the hands, in spite also of the monotony of the human features, this miniature and the others that accompany it attract us by the diversity and intensity of the action they describe, as well as by their coloring. The palette is not varied but the shades are warm and the shadows strongly modeled. The wall of the enclosure and its door in the foreground are very delicately painted.

The name of Jean Le Tavernier is once more put forward as the artist of this series of nine miniatures. We know, from documents, that he is the painter of numerous grisailles in a comparable style; we have also seen that he could have painted one (plate 28) series of miniatures in 1451 and perhaps a second one (plate 32) in 1455, using a diluted gouache similar to watercolor. The text from which this illustration is taken was composed by René d'Anjou in 1455; the Brussels copy, destined for Isabella of Portugal and Philip the Good, is probably only a little later than that date, since it was normal to present a work soon after it was completed, as an homage from the author. It is difficult to conceive, even though one may make comparisons among these miniatures, that Jean Le Tavernier could possibly have possessed such versatility as to work simultaneously in grisaille, in a kind of watercolor (in some ways very close to the grisaille), and in highly colored painting of the sort described above. Not only is this style of miniature different from that of the paintings ascribed with certainty to Le Tavernier, but neither does any other work of the Burgundian period resemble them. A deeper knowledge of the history of manuscripts would probably provide us with some useful elements to help us to reach a conclusion.

The frontispiece folio and one of the first pages of the text are both decorated with very special margins. Together with the broad, thickly painted acanthus leaves, we find in the lower margin the lozenge-shaped shield of Isabella of Portugal, third wife of Philip the Good, their initials *P* and *Y*, and the scroll bearing the motto *Tant que je vive* (As long as I live). The shield is planted in a "Hortus conclusus," symbol of virginity or the renunciation of the flesh. The right margin shows similar motifs of Philip the Good: his coat of arms with the necklace of the Golden Fleece, the motto *Aultre n'auray* (No other shall I have), the two *E*'s placed face to face, and his cry *Montjoye*. On the second of these two pages, in a very large initial, the coats of arms of the sovereign couple appear again, one above the other, attesting that the book was indeed intended for both of them, though individually; no other miniature has been preserved where this double ownership is presented so distinctly. On the first page, moreover, we find another heraldic motif twice: the shield of René d'Anjou, with its numerous divisions and pieces. It has been painted in the miniature itself and even in the initial at the beginning of the text, in the place where the coat of arms of the owner is usually painted. The most satisfying hypothesis explaining these three groups of blazons seems to be the following: René d'Anjou personally offered a copy of his work to the Duke and Duchess of Burgundy. In 1457 husband and wife parted from each other, in consequence of a difference over their son Charles the Bold. Isabella retired for some years to the Nieppe forest where she founded a convent of Grey Sisters. Did not the reconciliation of the duke and duchess provide René d'Anjou with an opportunity to send them his *Mortifiement de Vaine Plaisance*?

If René d'Anjou himself ordered this copy, as seems probable in view of the facts described, he could have had it decorated by Flemish illuminators or by miniaturists attached to his own court. It is not surprising therefore that the manuscript does not fall into conventional categories.

31

# The Punishment of the Rebellious Angels

JACQUES LE GRAND, Le Livre des bonnes mœurs. *Southern Netherlands. About 1455–1460.*
*65 folios (11$^3/_4$ × 8$^3/_4$"); 1 miniature with marginal decorations.*
*Ms. 11063, f. 3*

CHRIST IN MAJESTY or God surrounded by angels was a subject frequently used in painting and sculpture since the earliest Christian art. Some grandiose figurations of this theme have been preserved from the twelfth and thirteenth centuries, mainly on the portals of cathedrals. The theme has undergone important variants and has even come very close to a similar subject: the Creation and Fall of the Angels. The miniature reproduced here is a development of the latter, the iconography of which we have already admired in a series of six paintings on the frontispiece of a historiated Bible (plate 21). God the Father, clad in a magnificent cape, is seated in all His glory on a golden throne; the movement of His right hand suggests a blessing. The throne is in the monumental style we have already noticed in several other miniatures (plates 17 & 20), but the exaggerated width is not here so conspicuous, thanks to the generous folds of the mantle spread out on the seat. The artist did not trouble to paint its corner pillars in perspective: they are seen from the front. The painter of the Madonna "à la supplique" (plate 20) was not so neglectful. This faulty detail is unexpected from an artist so talented and original. He probably accepted the traditional architectural conception of the divine throne and merely reproduced it without concern for a law he otherwise knew perfectly.

The Divine Person is surrounded by concentric rings of angels painted in different colors. Three

Tous orgueilleux se veulent a dieu comparer En tant quilz se glorifient en eulx mesmes et es biens quilz ont Desquelles choses la gloire est deue principalment a

circles only are visible, but they are painted in such a way that we are under the impression that there are more – probably nine, one for each angel chorus – hidden behind the clouds and extending beyond the frame. This part of the picture, dazzling bright, appears above a whirlwind of black clouds swarming with devils and monsters. These heavy clouds rise from a chasm of dark rocks and opaque swamps, in the middle of which opens a crater aglow with incandescent lava. A devil larger than the others is hurled, head downward, into this pit. It is Satan thrust into Hell because of his arrogant rebellion. All the other devils are also flung down from Heaven; this indicates the moment of the punishment of the rebels, and not merely Hell as opposed to Heaven. The circles of angels, on the contrary, are quite static: we do not witness the desertion of some of them, nor their fall; they seem to be completely intent upon the adoration of God.

No medieval painting has rendered this iconography with such brilliancy and so much sense of grandeur. The distribution of the angels in these varicolored circles is a very effective innovation. The angels' heads, though barely indicated against a very light monochrome ground, are remarkably well modeled. They are all looking at God, toward whom they converge. Each circle is painted in a different tint so as to emphasize the impression of depth and volume already produced by the skillful arrangement. One could not give a better rendering of the multitude of the heavenly choirs.

The miniaturists were never great masters of the painting of clouds. Although the artist of Jean Chevrot's *City of God* had painted some clouds of great beauty, the purpose of these was purely decorative – they were there merely to break the monotony of the sky – whereas in this Punishment of Satan the clouds have a functional character that is indispensable to the vision of Hell imagined by the illuminator. In this respect we may well ask, what fifteenth-century painting can equal this page? It is here that the feeling of depth is rendered at its best. The painter had given his imagination full scope when he painted the grimacing and gesticulating devils in the infernal abyss. Another merit of this miniature is its coloring. The graded tints of the angels' circles and the dark grayish blue of the clouds have already been mentioned; the saffron yellow blended with red conveys remarkably well the refulgence of the angels around the divine throne and even more the glow of the flames in Hell.

The originality displayed in the theme, the composition, and the coloring attest the talent of a true master, in spite of a few shortcomings in perspective, and of the stiffness of the folds in God the Father's mantle. We shall shortly see (plate 35) an improved form of this rendering of God in Majesty surrounded by angels in the extraordinary illumination painted by Simon Marmion. For this reason alone, the hand of that artist could be suspected in this page as well. We must point out, however, a few stylistic differences. Simon Marmion, who executed several works we will analyze (plates 34, 35, and 38), is characterized by the gentleness in the appearance of his figures and by the very light shades of his coloring. In the only miniature of the *Livre des bonnes mœurs*, God the Father's features are strongly marked and His beard is very stiff. Of course the artist might by then have improved his style; but it is difficult to understand why Simon Marmion, after being so successful with dark coloring and the painting of clouds, did not return to those processes in which he had displayed such mastery. These remarks are tempered by caution, which is necessary as little or nothing is known of the working methods of a master illuminator and his atelier. In any case, the miniature reproduced here is pervaded with the personality of that painter from Valenciennes.

The spiritual meaning of this picture is a lesson that shows where vice and virtue ultimately lead, and no other representation of Heaven or Hell could have better illustrated this text. This conception of Hell is somewhere between that found in a page of *Les Très Riches Heures*, painted by the Limbourg brothers for Jean de Berry, and the fantastic visions of Hieronymus Bosch; it is closer, even, to the latter. Our illuminator must have been under the influence of a profound inspiration reminiscent of the vision of Dante himself. The manuscript bears the coat of arms of Croy; sufficient justice has not yet been done to this family's traditional interest in beautiful painted books at the time of the patronage of the dukes of Burgundy.

# The Dominican Brochard at Work

GUILLAUME ADAM, Ung advis pour faire le passage d'Oultremer, *translated by Jean Miélot. Lille. 1455.*
*699 folios ($15^1/_4 \times 10^5/_8$"); 3 large miniatures; manuscript written on paper.*
*Ms. 9095, f. 1*

A SCRIBE in the very act of writing may often be represented in medieval manuscripts, sometimes a scribe who is at the same time the author composing and copying his text. It is not always easy to know which figure is shown, although the key to the problem is generally found in the context. Sometimes, the author and the scribe are seen together in the same picture. The first and the most ancient of the pages reproduced in the present book (plate 1) offers one of the most impressive examples of this theme, which dates back to the Roman period. In another miniature (plate 8), we have a sacred author, the Evangelist Matthew; while in the preceding one (plate 6) we see a scribe holding the tablets on which he is going to write at the dictation of the author, St. Gregory the Great. We will see later how these representations are revealing of the times in which they were painted.

It is an author, assuredly, who is presented to us in the frontispiece folio of this manuscript; probably we have preserved no medieval picture expounding the theme so fully. Here we really see the author in the very act of composing his work. He is busy writing in a manuscript which is, for the moment, lying on his knee; if we look at the wide-open books around him, we see that this is the only one with an unfinished right-hand page. Has the author removed from the desk the book in which he was writing, and laid it aside for a while in order to consult another,

or was he transcribing his own text into the manuscript on his knee, in a rather uncomfortable position? This last suggestion should not be rejected. If it were the case, we would assume that the author had discontinued his work and had also turned his seat around, as in his present position it would be impossible for him to write at the desk. Is he shown at the very moment he stopped writing, now pondering whether to consult a necessary text before continuing his own, or is he about to dip his pen quite mechanically into the inkstand on the chest which supports the desk? It cannot be that such a gifted and scrupulous artist as the painter of this frontispiece would have made a drawing that corresponds to no actual situation. The presence of large folios scattered over the floor may seem to contradict this assertion, but they are there for the sake of filling the empty space which was so distasteful to medieval painters. With this in mind, we are surprised that the wall in the background should have been left without ornaments. Their absence increases the importance of the lamp hanging over the desk. A last detail shows the accuracy of our artist: the back of the room is filled by a kind of sofa on which lie an open manuscript and a loosely folded rug. The sofa has a hinged back that can pivot lengthwise as desired. Of course, this piece of furniture plays no special part in the scene; it only shows the painter's concern for accuracy both in small details and in his principal subject.

The author in the picture wears the Dominican habit. In the preface Jean Miélot, the translator, ascribes this *Advis pour faire le passage d'Oultremer* to a German monk called Brochard, of the order of St. Dominic. The figure represented here is not Jean Miélot, as generally believed, nor is it Brochard, for he is no longer accepted as the author of the text. It is now thought to be one William Adams, who may have written it when he returned from the Near East, where he had journeyed to "preach the Christian faith." The subject of this work is related to the sudden wave of interest in the East that flooded Europe in the middle of the fifteenth century, which we have already mentioned in connection with the *Débat sur l'honneur* (plate 28). Constantinople had just fallen, the alarm had been sounded, and all Christendom was talking of starting a crusade. Philip the Good, who was at that time the most powerful prince in the Occident, was already making active preparations in view of the proposed campaign. In 1454, he assembled in Lille the dignitaries of all his States for a sumptuous feast during which he made them take an oath and swear that they would take part in the crusade. This is the famous "Vow of the Pheasant." A few months later, in 1455, Jean Miélot had completed the translation of his text which, in the meantime, came to have general interest. Let us recall that at that time Miélot was established in Lille. From 1449 to 1454, he had been with the court as a scribe attached to the personal suite of the duke for whom he adapted or translated texts concerned with spiritual life. His activities during that period have already been mentioned twice (plate 22, the addition to the Prayer Book of the Duke of Burgundy, and plate 28, the *Débat sur l'honneur*). He was rewarded for his many services with a canon's prebendaryship in St. Peter's church in Lille. From that time on he used his new title in the prefaces of his numerous works, and his books were written on paper rather than on parchment.

Several painters, illuminators, and decorators were invited to Lille on account of the Pheasant festival; among them was Jean Le Tavernier. The miniatures decorating the *Débat sur l'honneur* (plate 28), executed in 1451, have been ascribed to him for different reasons, one of them being that their watercolor style resembles the grisaille typical of this illuminator. The same argument cannot be so convincingly put forward in the present case for, as early as 1454, Jean Le Tavernier had already established his reputation as a master of grisaille, in the Book of Hours of Philip the Good. We find again, however, in the miniature reproduced here, the same watercolor process and the same dominant tone of blue as in the *Débat sur l'honneur*. The gold glaze has disappeared, perhaps with the evolution of the technique; but when one comes to analyze the rendering of the faces it is hardly possible to make a valid comparison between this large figure in our miniature and the numerous small figures in the procession of the *Débat sur l'honneur*. In view of these known facts, the attribution to Jean Le Tavernier remains the most tenable, or if not to him, at least to one of his close assistants.

Several plates of this volume have already shown the theme of the author sitting at his desk as he writes. The earliest (plate 1) is marked with a classicism that will not appear again; in the two others (plates 6 & 8), both the author and the scribe have the honor of being represented because of the religious text they have composed or copied: they have participated in a work dedicated to God. In this later miniature the painter has been content to represent an author struggling with his problems. The anecdotic and human character of this page is a welcome sign of the recent enrichment of the artist's sensitivity.

## 33 Scenes from the Life of the Virgin

JEAN MANSEL, La Fleur des Histoires, *first part. Northern France. 1455–60.*
*490 folios (17¹/₈ × 11³/₄"); 42 miniatures with marginal decorations.*
*Ms. 9231, f. 179*

THOUGH THE MIDDLE AGES had a liking for mannered symbolism, it nevertheless preferred the anecdote, the picture that tells a story. In the heyday of the painted manuscript, there was always a craving for illustrations, which for that reason were called "histoires." The Burgundian period was, perhaps more than any other, the golden age of the book adorned with pictures illustrating the text. One could hardly find a more brilliant example than this miniature in which the artist has so pleasantly assembled the principal moments of the Virgin's life before she was called to her part in the drama of the Saviour. The scenes, beginning at the top left corner and descending on the left-hand side, continue around the miniature and finally end at the starting point. St. Anne, the wife of Joachim, is quietly walking in her garden when she hears from the Archangel Gabriel that, in spite of her advanced age, she will conceive a daughter *qui moult saincte seroit* (who will be very holy). On the celestial messenger's advice, she goes to Jerusalem where she meets her husband at the Golden Gate. Some time after, St. Anne bears a child. The birth is watched over by an angel. A few years later, *quand Marie avait trois ans* (when Mary was three years old) – says the author – the parents brought their daughter to the temple in Jerusalem *où elle monta sans l'ayde d'autruin* (where she walked up alone). Mary entered God's service, and thenceforth prayed and embroidered vestments. We see her kneeling

in a chapel close to the temple, which is the large building with a cupola on the right side of the picture.

The illuminator has faithfully followed the text of *La Fleur des Histoires*. The author, Jean Mansel, had previously proved his interest in historical works by translating and adapting the work of Livy in his own *Histoires Romaines*. *La Fleur des Histoires* is, as its name indicates, a compilation of familiar stories concerning the events of the past. The Old and the New Testament occupy a choice place in this vast panorama. Some of the facts of St. Anne's life described in this chapter and reproduced in the pictures are inspired by the Apocrypha: the Proto-Gospel of James and the Pseudo-Gospel of Matthew.

Miniatures of this kind – and there are many in our manuscript as well as in the others coming from the same workshop – offer an incredibly rich iconographic content. There is no superfluity and every detail is treated with equal care; some of the scenes are allowed more and some less space, depending on their importance in the cycle of pictures. In the center is the birth of the Virgin, the principal part of the miniature. It is one of the most unsophisticated indoor scenes of medieval painting to have been preserved for us. There is no affectation here, but keen observation of objects, attitudes, and gestures; the details have the flavor of real life. The seats are identical and their red cushions are covered with green tapestry bearing Christ's monogram. We see the sideboard with the mother's meal prepared in advance, the gesture of the servant sprinkling the infant's body with water, and the pensive attitude of the mother. What words could describe the fond gesture of Anne and Joachim rejoicing at the coming of the child? Better still, the true-to-life attitude of the maid drawing water from the river? This lovely though irrelevant little scene in the entrance of a courtyard is absolutely unrelated to the subject, but adds a touch of fantasy that we welcome in this artist, otherwise so scrupulous in his exactitude. Let us notice, moreover, that Anne and Joachim wear mantles of the same color in all the pictures, enabling us to identify them at first glance. Mary, once she is in the temple, wears garments suitable to her new way of life. These are details, but they bear witness to the artist's rare conscientiousness in the art of illustrating a text.

The pictorial quality of this large-size miniature is just as rich as its narrative value. Nothing is overlooked, everything is painted in bold colors coming from a palette that seems to have unlimited resources. The landscape, barely seen through a small gap in the building, is painted in delicate tints which become softer as they fade away toward the distant horizon. The artist of the miniature we have just described painted most of the pictures in the first part of *La Fleur des Histoires* written by Jean Mansel, hence his anonymous appellation as the Master of Mansel. He was the principal collaborator, at least for a while, of an important workshop in the north of France, perhaps in Arras, Valenciennes or Cambrai, or even Amiens. For his compilation,

Jean Mansel made use of Jean Wauquelin's texts written between 1448 and 1450. His work is thus later than that date. The transcription and the decoration of this first volume perhaps were made about 1455.

In the varied production that appears during the reign of Philip the Good, the manuscripts in which we find the hand of the Master of Mansel are the most French in style. The "bastard" handwriting is small and fine; it shows a quite different conception of the art of the letter than the so-called Burgundian bastard hand. The margins, too, are French, with their graceful scroll foliage, their fine gold ornaments, and their various floral decorations. In fact, the style of this painter continues that of the Master of Bedford, whose talent had prevailed in the Parisian production around 1430. We find this strikingly confirmed in the frontispiece miniature of the first volume of *La Fleur des Histoires:* it is an absolutely identical reproduction of the six pictures depicting the Creation and Fall of the Angels, executed in Paris around 1410 (plate 21). We cannot suppose the Master of Mansel copied the miniature out of the Historiated Bible, since *La Fleur des Histoires* did not come to the Burgundian Library until much later. Probably a workshop cartoon bearing color indications accounts for the identical drawing and the almost identical quality after an interval of forty years.

How did this manuscript in two volumes (plate 34) come into the duke's library? It is unthinkable that a work of this quality would show no sign of its first owner if it had been ordered by Philip the Good himself. It was therefore executed for some other book collector from whom it was acquired for the duke's collection. William Fillastre, bishop of Tournai, who seems never to have put his mark on his books, could have been the owner of this incomparable copy. He lost his property and library to the benefit of Charles the Bold, in 1465. We will examine this question again when we come to another manuscript (plate 38) that contributes a valuable point to this hypothesis.

## 34 Episodes in the Life of Charles V

JEAN MANSEL, La Fleur des Histoires, *second part. Northern France. About 1455–60.*
*490 folios (17 1/8 × 11 3/4"); 24 miniatures with marginal decorations.*
*Ms. 9232, f. 423*

AS IN THE PICTURE devoted to Mary's childhood, the painter has grouped together five episodes from the life of Charles V of Valois, who reigned over France from 1364 to 1380. Their order, opposite from that in the preceding plate, reads diagonally upward from the lower right. A procession of court dignitaries and ladies of high rank are attending the marriage in 1350 of Charles, son of John the Good and future King of France, to Joanna of Bourbon. On the left, under an imaginary but beautifully designed building, Charles V is crowned king by the Archbishop Jean de Craon, in Reims (1364). The king and queen are seen from behind, both dressed in blue and each wearing a crown. Again on the right we have the alms-giving on the occasion of the birth of the dauphin, in 1368, who will succeed his father twelve years later as Charles VI. A member of the palace staff is welcoming the poor and handing them silver coins taken from a casket that is held open by a servant. At the window a nurse presents the dauphin to the people: the infant's mantle is embroidered with the emblem of France. Higher up is one of the numerous battles the king fought during his reign, and lastly, toward the left-hand side, an episode of the Hundred Years War, in which the English troops set fire to a fortress on their way across France.

The miniature described above illustrates one of the last quires of the second volume of *La*

Le roy charles le
quint et la royne

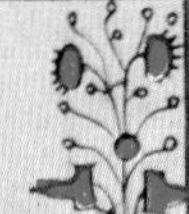

plusieurs ducs contes et barons puis
vindrent a paris a grant honneur

*Fleur des Histoires*, written by Jean Mansel. It was painted by a different artist from the one responsible for the preceding plate, but shows at first glance the strength of the tradition in the same workshop. Indeed, though this second illuminator was rather more talented than the previous one, he was obliged also to conform to the general conception imposed by the publisher of the book.

This restraint did not, however, prevent the painter from asserting himself as a master in composition and coloring. Gaps of several years actually separate the five subjects of the miniature, but these are so skillfully blended that we are inclined to think they deal with one theme only. The wedding, for instance, with its procession of beautiful ladies, takes place on the steps of a sanctuary inside which, fourteen years later, the bishop crowns the king. The distribution of alms to the poor, eighteen years later, is indistinguishable from the rest: on the right, at the bottom of the picture, an arch heightens the illusion of continuity in the theme by attracting attention to the very window in which we see the child. Lastly, in the exact center of the picture, a door has been left open in the enclosure wall, inviting us to search further. The composition of this picture is undeniably effective, mainly because it compels the eye to follow obliquely, from one side to the other, the scenes which alternate toward the top of the miniature: from the white-mantled lady in the lower right, to the bishop crowning the king, across to the dauphin, and then to the English soldiers at the top left-hand corner.

Not only has the new illustrator of *La Fleur des Histoires* rendered more supple the somewhat geometrical distribution of his predecessor and master, but the tints of his palette also show more gradation than those of the Master of Mansel, rich and varied though these were. We can feel his preference for the more delicate shades; it is in the juxtaposition of colors, however, that he asserts himself as an incomparable master, for these are always pleasantly contrasted while retaining all their individual charm. This master, moreover, must have used his brush with the utmost delicacy to obtain such exquisite shading without any loss of distinctness.

The two main qualities of our painter – composition and coloring – should not lead us to overlook the progress he has made in the rendering of the faces. Their features are excellently modeled; the artist prefers the pink and fleshy type, but always preserves a striking individuality. The women are also painted according to a canon that the artist has chosen himself; in comparison with others from pictures of that time, they display a rare elegance. There is no question, however, of making a comparison between the faces in this miniature with those in the frontispiece of the *Chroniques de Hainaut* (plate 27) which is an unparalleled specimen, its exceptionally high quality being due to the very high rank of its owner. The present illumination, grouping episodes of the life of Charles V, is merely one miniature among others of equivalent quality; it is a workshop production. The progress it shows bears witness to a personal talent, but it also reveals the aesthetic development in the workshop of a more discerning taste, thus making it an important landmark in the history of illumination in the Low Countries.

Critics are unanimous in ascribing to Simon Marmion this illustration of the life of Charles V and the other illuminations decorating the latter part of the manuscript. No written evidence supports this attribution, but the historical and stylistic arguments in its favor are such that it would be difficult to oppose.

Jean Le Maire, in characterizing Simon Marmion among the other Burgundian artists, calls him *le prince d'enluminure* (the prince of illuminators) and thus attests for the fame of this artist in his lifetime. Modern critics agree with this appreciation, for no other atelier produced, during the reign of Philip the Good, any miniatures comparable in quality with those left to us by this artist.

The collaboration of Simon Marmion in the second book of *La Fleur des Histoires* poses certain problems. In the first part he is so faithful a disciple of the Master of Mansel that it is not easy to discern one hand from the other. This volume does certainly show new features indicating Marmion, but these do not yet bear the stamp of the master. After several quires without illustrations the great Marmion appears at his best, toward the end of this second part, in miniatures of the quality reproduced here. Did the Master of Mansel die during the production of these volumes, thus leaving Marmion at liberty to assert his own style, or did the probable owner of this manuscript (plate 33), William Fillastre, delay the decoration of his copy so as to entrust it entirely to his protégé? It is to be feared that this problem will never be solved. Since the style of this last part is more evolved, it is likely that these later miniatures were painted about 1460. In 1458, Marmion settled in Valenciennes and may there have collaborated with colleagues from the atelier in which the Master of Mansel worked: thus the hypothesis proposed in the previous description, concerning the localizing of the atelier in Valenciennes, would be confirmed.

## 35 The Garden of Eden

LES SEPT AGES DU MONDE. *Probably Mons. About 1460.*
*350 folios ($17^1/_8 \times 12''$); 2 large miniatures; 1 small miniature; marginal decorations.*
*Ms. 9047, f. 1 v*

THE PARADISIAC THEME of the Garden of Eden must have frightened many a medieval artist, for its representation is seldom encountered in manuscripts. The six days of the Creation have often been described in separate pictures, mainly in Bibles, but only a few painters have represented the Seventh Day, when God, beholding his work, declares Himself satisfied with what He has done. In a miniature belonging to the *Très Riches Heures de Jean de Berry*, preserved in Chantilly, which may with full justice be called incomparable for its time, the Limbourg brothers have painted one of the most poetical images of Paradise, but they have included two episodes from the Genesis story: the Fall of Man and the Expulsion. In the miniature reproduced on the opposite plate, on the contrary, the painter has contrived to make us participate in the greatness and beauty of this capital moment in the cosmogony, as imagined with all the sensitiveness of the Middle Ages.

God the Father, in all His majesty, is blessing the world He has just created. He is seated on a large throne and holds in His hand the golden globe surmounted with a cross, symbol of universal sovereignty. Grouped in concentric circles in the radiance of His glory, angels adore the Divinity. To separate the divine universe – if it can so be called – from the rest of creation, the illuminator has painted another colored circle in gradations from dark blue to white. Immediately

Dieux le souverain
commencemens est
lumiere parfaite.
en quoy toutes
choses visibles et
invisibles passees presentes et ad

mouvement dair. Et saches que
dieu est sa parolle et sa parolle est
dieu. Et est ceste parolle complie
et parfaite par iii. souveraines
dignites sans lesquelles dignites
la parolle dieu cest a dire la deite

beyond yet still in the same group of concentric designs, stars are shining against the dark background of the celestial vault. The latter is supported by the seven heavens, represented by seven pale blue bands in each of which shines one heavenly body. The moon belongs to the lowest sphere, and has the usual crescent form. The lower part of the picture is devoted to the terrestrial universe. The painter has separated the waters from the earth, thus keeping close to the text in Genesis describing the third day of the Creation: "Let the waters under the heaven be gathered together unto one place, and let the dry land appear." And God said, "Let the earth bring forth grass . . . and the fruit tree yielding fruit after his kind . . . ." The fifth day God decided: "Let the waters bring forth . . . fowl that may fly above the earth in the open firmament of heaven," and the sixth day "God made the beast of the earth after his kind," after which God created Man in His own image and told him that the universe was at his disposal.

The author of the picture has endeavored to condense the essential facts of the Creation; he has magnified God the Creator and expounded the theme of the creation of light and firmament; in the description of the Garden of Eden he had the good taste to simplify the figuration: a few animals; a flight of birds in the sky, others resting on the sea; and, at last, Adam and Eve in a landscape with a few trees. The first human beings, represented nude and overwhelmed under the immensity of the skies by God's majesty, are profoundly pathetic and yet impregnated with a true sense of grandeur. Moreover, this picture displays a freshness and lyricism much in advance of its time. How alive and human are the simple attitudes of our first parents: Adam confidently approaching Eve who answers with a charming gesture of flattered coquetry! And how peaceful is this stag, drinking from the river with both his forelegs in the water! The whole composition would have been a failure had Adam and Eve occupied the center of the miniature; it would indeed have been poor taste to build the whole page on its medial line. The lower part of the picture is, fortunately, conceived on an axis from right to left – from the sea, with its level horizon, to Adam and Eve, the heart of the subject, in the lower left of the miniature. Here, then, is another composition on the diagonal line such as we have already encountered (plate 34); it is, besides, ascribed to the same miniaturist, Simon Marmion. He once more asserts his originality in the art of composing a page as well as his mastery in the use of color; the latter is displayed in his very personal use of warm and subtle tints which we recognize at once and can consider to be his signature. Also, this miniature shows a new stage in the artistic development of the painter: he is now able to represent a subject which is not merely anecdotic but in a new way abstract; he has expressed here all the profundity of its theological and human significance.

The miniature, which is a representation of the Creation at the moment of its completion, is the frontispiece illustration of a little-known text: *Les sept âges du monde* (*The Seven Ages of the World*). The prologue, in which the author might have disclosed his name, has been removed from the book, probably because it was also decorated with a miniature as beautiful as this one. The principal theme of this anonymous text is God and his creative actions. The author's intention was to introduce to the uninitiated public some theological problems arising from Genesis. The transcription of this highly spiritual work, which is perhaps the only copy to have been preserved, was executed in the well-known workshop of Jacquemart Pilavaine. First a scribe, Pilavaine later became a publisher in Mons where he succeeded Jean Wauquelin in 1452. It seems that he himself wrote all of this copy of *The Seven Ages of the World*, for his typical handwriting – the most elaborate Burgundian bastard type – is easily recognizable. The few marginal decorations reproduced on the plate are also typical of his atelier. Besides, the manuscript belonged to and was even ordered by a member of the Croy family, the faithful protectors of the Mons workshop. Their coat of arms appears in the initial under the miniature.

We thus see in a manuscript executed in Mons, the hand of a painter whose main production was the illustration of books that were made in another atelier situated in a town of northern France. One might feel inclined to suggest that the manuscript was taken from Mons to receive elsewhere the miniatures that were to decorate it; but the examination of the marginal decorations reveals Marmion's presence in Pilavaine's very workshop, because the techniques typical of each master are coexistent in the manuscript. The copy of *The Seven Ages of the World* preserved in Brussels is thus a very interesting case: it shows that the archaeology of the medieval book is indispensable to the history of illumination. In it we can follow Marmion's movements and therefore explain the influence of his style.

36

# King Godfrey of Denmark Giving Audience to the Four Envoys of Charlemagne

DAVID AUBERT, Chroniques et Conquêtes de Charlemagne, *vol. I. Southern Netherlands. The transcription was finished in 1458; the illuminator, Jean Le Tavernier, was paid for the miniatures in 1460.*
*453 folios (16 1/2 × 11 5/8"); 42 miniatures in grisaille.*
*Ms. 9066, f. 169 v*

THE CAPTION under this miniature gives the most important information about the picture; for the better understanding of the scene, however, it is preferable to recall a few details of the legend illustrated here. The Emperor Charlemagne had attacked and defeated King Godfrey of Denmark who, for the past ten years, had refused him obedience. Both sides stopped fighting on Godfrey's promise that he would join the other vassals in rendering homage to the emperor at Easter. As a sign of fidelity he pledged his son Ogier. Betraying his word, "Godfrey of Dampnemarche," as the author calls him, did not appear at the assembly of the great vassals of the Empire. Charlemagne, infuriated, was on the verge of putting young Ogier to death in accordance with the agreement, but, on second thoughts, decided that such an action was unworthy of him, especially on such a day. On his councilors' advice he sent four messengers to threaten the father with Ogier's death and the loss of the kingdom of Denmark, if he failed to keep his word. The miniature shows these envoys being brought to the dining hall where Godfrey and his wife are having their meal. The text adds that the King of Denmark had delayed their entrance, for *il avait le courage moult felon* (his heart was very traitorous) and he feared bad news. He finally received them unbecomingly and sent them back to the emperor, after having insulted them outrageously. The valiant Ogier owed his life to the intervention of the Archbishop of Mainz; but his father received the fate he deserved.

omer Si se tait a tant listoire de ce et dist.

Comment charlemaine enuoia ses messaiges deuers gauffroy de dampnemarche lesqlz Il fist deffigurer ou despit de lempereur.

The fragment of the legend that the miniaturist chose to illustrate is so lavishly represented that, from being a mere anecdote, the picture becomes a scene of real life. The effect of the perfect symmetry of the composition is to draw attention to the central part of the painting showing the king and queen at dinner, after which one sees the numerous details that contribute to the enlivening of the main action – at first we do not notice the emperor's envoys delivering their message to the King of Denmark. A parallel can be established between the conception of the illustration painted by the illuminator of the *Chroniques et Conquêtes de Charlemagne*, and that of the painter of the 1431 Dutch Bible (plate 24). Both take advantage of the theme provided by the text, to enlarge it and put it directly on a more human scale. Our illustrator, who was not afraid of painting masses of people, seems to have crowded the picture for sheer pleasure. On the right of the royal couple are knights and soldiers; on their left, dignitaries and councilors. Numerous servants come and go across the hall: the cup-bearer standing near the richly garnished sideboard, the servant bringing in the dishes, and another serving at the table give liveliness to the picture. Two dogs fill the small space left in the foreground. The person standing behind the fourth kneeling messenger might be Guyon, son of Godfrey by his second wife; the king had summoned him just before the envoys' arrival. The strictly geometrical perspective does not in the least impair the attractiveness of this thrilling scene. In order to increase the impression of depth, the painter has used an illusionistic process which consists of presenting the subject as if it were seen through a large opening made in the wall. This is why a frame of bricks has been painted on three sides of the picture.

We know the author and copyist of the text: he is David Aubert, who declares he completed his work in 1458. From the accounts found in the archives of the princely court of Burgundy, we learn that in March, 1460, "Jean Le Tavernier, illuminator in Audenarde" received a payment for some *Histoires* in black and white that he made in this first volume of the *Chroniques et Conquêtes de Charlemagne*. Although Le Tavernier seldom adopts such a symmetrical distribution in his paintings, the miniature reproduced here is a valuable testimonial of his talent. Refusing to indulge in the charm of color, he preferred the metallic sobriety of grisaille. A passionate lover of action, his firm, clear-cut drawings of those "scenes from life" illustrate the themes which he found in the texts; his pictures often make a better narrative than do the stories themselves.

Le Tavernier made the best possible use of grisaille, which allows very contrasted modeling. He painted with verve and succeeded in creating a characteristic human type recognizable by its thin bony face and well-marked features. All figures take an active part in the scene, as we see from their slightly emphasized gestures, and they produce a general effect not conveyed in other miniatures. Each of these pictures is a little world peopled by puppets who live in a veritable whirlwind. The grisaille of Le Tavernier is not like that of the other samples of this technique reproduced in the present book. In the Paris Missal (plate 17) and in the Hours of Jean de Berry (plates 19 & 20) we have observed that such beautifully graduated shades of a single color have been obtained only by using extraordinary delicacy in the application of the color wash. In the Entombment, in the Dutch Book of Hours (plate 25), the grisaille seems to have been made with extremely fine touches of the silverpoint pencil, distributed more or less thickly as the case demanded and managed with exceptional skill. The Audenarde painter, on the contrary, makes use of two shades of gouache, black and white, distributed according to the dark and light surfaces. Le Tavernier's sensitiveness to movement is also shown by his vigorous application of the pigments.

As in most medieval works, the contents of the *Chroniques et Conquêtes de Charlemagne* are not entirely new. David Aubert drew part of his inspiration from the massive production of another publisher, Jean Wauquelin, who had specialized in historical texts. Aubert was asked by Jean de Créquy to compose this story of Charlemagne; he states the fact in his prologue. However, the manuscript was not completed for this brilliant soldier of Philip the Good; the payment for the miniature was made to Jean Le Tavernier by the Duke of Burgundy's paymaster. The copy, moreover, opens on a frontispiece folio decorated with a very large miniature bearing the mark of the new owner. This must be the result of a substitution cleverly inserted in the manuscript.

The works of Jean Le Tavernier that have come down to us are impressive in number. The Book of Hours of Philip the Good, now in the Royal Library of The Hague, was unfortunately deprived of a fair number of its miniatures following an alteration made about 1475. There are still preserved two superb copies of *Les Miracles de Notre Dame*, one of which was executed shortly after the Book of Hours. The three volumes of the *Chroniques et Conquêtes de Charlemagne* remain, nevertheless, Jean Le Tavernier's undisputed masterpiece. In the references to him or to his work that we find in the Duke of Burgundy's accounts, he is always mentioned as "an inhabitant of Audenarde"; it is therefore probable that this illuminator never attached himself to any particular publisher but put his craftmanship at the disposal of those who paid him best. The mastery he had acquired in this original technique of grisaille perhaps allowed him to be more independent than the other illuminators.

37

# Christ Before Pilate

BOOK OF HOURS OF MARY VAN VRONENSTEYN. *Utrecht. 1460.*
*251 folios (5 × 5 1/2"); 12 large miniatures; several historiated initials of varying sizes; marginal decorations.*
*Ms. II 7619, f. 38 v*

CHRIST BEFORE PILATE is a recurrent scene in books of hours; it is one of the eight miniatures illustrating the Passion. Presented as it is in this miniature, however, this well-known subject arouses fresh interest. Such is the quality of the painting that one notices its rich vitality before thinking of the theme it represents.

The picture itself needs no commentary: it depicts the moment of the Passion when Jesus was lead by the Jews to be sentenced before Pilate. The Roman governor found no charge against Him according to the imperial law. His wife then came to warn him that she had been tormented by a dream and begged him to have no hand in the condemnation of this man. In spite of the warning, the menacing insistence of the Jews prevailed and Pilate delivered Jesus to them: "he took water, and washed his hands ... saying, I am innocent of the blood of this just person." The iconography is thus derived from Matthew's Gospel (27 : 24), for he is the only evangelist to mention the wife of Pilate as well as the washing of the hands.

Looking at this small picture it is difficult to decide what appeals to us most. The great dignity of Christ is immensely moving. According to the Gospel, Pilate was so impressed that he could not bring himself to find Him guilty of any offence and in his heart did not want to comply with the Jews' demand. The embarrassment of the Roman governor is admirably expressed too:

the look in his eyes denotes clearly that he is ashamed of his weak behavior and of the decision he is about to make; his right hand is half-raised in sign of regret, while the other is already reaching toward the basin of water, thus showing his consent. The bearing and gestures of Pilate's wife eloquently express the confidential character of their talk and her affectionate insistence on gaining her husband's attention. Never before in the Middle Ages has feminine charm been expressed with so much grace. The originality of this picture lies not only in the elegance of the clothes and the loveliness of the woman's face; it is her very soul the miniaturist has contrived to communicate. His psychological approach gives a foretaste of seventeenth-century Dutch "Intimism."

The knowledge of the human soul displayed in this moving description of the encounter of Christ with Pilate should not prevent our noting that some minor aspects are equally felicitous in this picture. Can we remain unmoved by the proud bearing of the servant who, on one knee, offers the basin to his master? Even the soldiers, each with a hand on their prisoner's arm, seem to understand the gravity of the moment and the importance of their duty. The surroundings in which the fate of Christ is decided are painted with similar care. The elaborate architecture of the throne and the hall is drawn, like the rest, in a free and easy manner, and this in spite of a very bold perspective. The subject is seen from the right side, with the light coming from the left and passing through a doorway into a neighboring room at the extreme right of the picture. The miniaturist has made the mistake, however, of framing his subject with the motif of an arch, as did Jean Le Tavernier (plate 36): a frame of this kind requires a perspective with the rays of light focused on the center of the picture, and the painter has thus been led to draw the tile flooring along an axis which is not parallel with the walls of the hall. Fortunately the grouping of people makes this confusion in the placement of the focus less noticeable.

The full-page miniature described above is one of twelve illuminated folios which are not, strictly speaking, part of a book of hours. In accordance with the Dutch custom, the miniatures were painted on the left-hand page of separate folios which were then set in the manuscript just before completion. The painter's contribution to the book was limited to these pictures and to their beautiful margins. The remaining decoration is the work of three illuminators, two of whom were remarkably gifted, though they cannot compare with the principal master. Unfortunately, the latter is unknown; he is styled somewhat tentatively the Master of Soudenbalch, because he illustrated a Bible for a person called by that name (now in the National Library in Vienna). The book of hours he has here decorated was owned by Mary van Vronensteyn, about whom no information has yet come to light. The chronological table added to the beginning of the book allows us to state that the manuscript was practically complete in 1460. From the calendar we learn that the Book of Hours is for the use of the bishopric of Utrecht; the style of the miniatures and even the decorative techniques of the book attest that it was made in that very town.

Around 1450, in the northern Netherlands, the art of manuscript illumination underwent a period of lesser brilliance in consequence of the Duke of Burgundy's conquest, which swept away the local patronage. Toward 1460, however, there is to be seen a revival in quality and even in luxury, that seems to coincide with the arrival to the episcopal throne of Utrecht, in 1457, of David of Burgundy, one of Philip the Good's numerous natural sons. The decoration in the Hours of Vronensteyn can be compared in quality with that in the Burgundian manuscripts; they even surpass the latter by the variety of styles they display. We have already stated that owing to the absence of an influential and exacting patronage, the artists of the northern Netherlands were less restricted. As a result, the Dutch miniaturists could retain not only their own manner but also their personal aesthetic values; they were not, as in other countries, more or less compelled to adopt the fashion imposed by the leaders of the ateliers. No wonder then that we should find side by side in the Dutch manuscripts miniatures of totally different style and quality. It is evident that a certain discrimination reigned over the Hours of Vronensteyn: the best of the four painters was chosen to do all of the twelve large miniatures, and nothing more. He is, no doubt, the most brilliant exponent of the Utrecht school for the years around 1460, while still remaining faithful to the traditional Dutch illumination. This tradition showed, earlier than the others, a concern for human values: the lifelike faces, the activities of daily life with their accompanying emotions. Its illuminators told of human sentiments and therefore did not content themselves with merely translating texts into pictures; they painted also the psychological reactions concerned in these events. We could find no better proof than in this encounter between Christ and Pilate, painted by the Master of Soudenbalch.

38

# The Crucifixion

PONTIFICAL OF THE CATHEDRAL OF SENS. *France. About 1400. Several miniatures added about 1460 in the southern Netherlands.*
*161 folios ($13^3/_4 \times 9^7/_8$"); 2 large miniatures; 19 historiated initials.*
*Ms. 9215, f. 129*

IN LITURGICAL BOOKS of a certain standing an illustration of Christ on the Cross always precedes the Canon, which is the group of prayers recited before and after the Consecration. The Pontifical is such a book containing all the liturgical texts for the sole use of the bishop, as well as the common prayers of the Mass. So it is normal to find in this manuscript, at the *Te igitur*, a miniature showing Christ on the Cross, with His mother, John the Evangelist and others. Although it was made around 1400, the Pontifical for the Cathedral of Sens shows at this place, for reasons to be explained later, a picture in true Flemish style, the very small proportions of which do not impair its exceptional beauty. The work of a painter who is also a miniaturist, this page is indubitable proof that illumination is not a minor form of art.

Almost all the figures standing on either side of Christ are those usually found in representations of this theme. At the right of Christ stand John, the mother of Jesus, and two holy women; on the left, two important Jews and a Roman soldier. The Gospel tells of three women who, with Jesus' mother, were at the Crucifixion: Mary Magdalen, Mary the mother of James and Joseph, and Salome the "mother of the sons of Zebedee." This Pontifical shows only two women. Such lack of accuracy is typical of the milieu from which the artist of this painting comes. His main concern, moreover, seems to be for the landscape. In Dutch

paintings, by contrast (particularly in the Hours of Mary van Vronensteyn), the miniaturists would not have been so at variance with the sacred text of the Gospel. Jesus has just "given up the spirit," and a Roman soldier has pierced His side with a spear to make sure He is really dead; only the Gospel of John mentions this. The beloved disciple seems appalled at his Master's death; he nevertheless supports Mary who would otherwise collapse with grief. Mary Magdalen is kneeling at the foot of the cross which she does not embrace, contrary to current iconography. In this group of Christ and His faithful disciples, the halo is replaced by a discreet rayed nimbus. Moreover, this is one of those rare painters sufficiently knowledgeable to write the text in three languages onto the scroll that is nailed above the cross: "Jesus of Nazareth, King of the Jews."

The group to the left of Christ is less easy to identify. The helmeted character on the far right of the picture is apparently a Roman soldier; he might be either the man who pierced Christ's side, or the centurion who confessed his faith after the earthquake that followed the death of Christ. This soldier seems to inveigh vehemently against a dignitary who also wears armor, his haughty bearing showing his satisfaction at the death of the Master. The most satisfactory interpretation is that one of them is the Roman centurion who confessed the divinity of the Crucified, the other is one of the Jewish elders who came to make sure of the victim's death.

Looking at this dramatic scene we could easily forget the landscape, but no master of Flemish illumination has ever given his painting a more beautiful background. Among the illustrations reproduced in the present publication there is only one of such beauty: the frontispiece folio of *The City of God* (plate 26). In the latter the landscape is simple, unsophisticated, and very real; that of the Crucifixion is more elaborate and varied, its scenery certainly drawn from life but the general effect more conventional. Several other miniatures by the same master show the town with its gate flanked by two large towers, and its belfry and cathedral, which here decorates the extreme left of the picture.

We recognize at once the hand of Simon Marmion. His talent has developed, but seems to have been slightly influenced by the fashion of the moment. The faces are tremendously individual and he has even dared to give Christ, who has died after atrocious suffering, the appearance of a real corpse. All the details are carefully observed. The anatomy, the wounds, and the blood flowing from the crucified body are highly realistic. The light, the rippling water of the river, the undulating hills, the rows of trees in the distance, all are rendered with the same accuracy. There is to be found in this painting a sense of the pathetic not encountered in Marmion's previous works. On the other hand, the exaggerated manifestations of sorrow by the Virgin and St. John are the opposite extreme of the restrained dignity of Adam and Eve in the Garden of Eden (plate 35).

The expression of human feelings, especially of the deepest ones such as this mother's grief, has always been the touchstone of a painter's talent. Marmion was not unable to express them, but, influenced by his time and his surroundings – the Burgundian court at the peak of its wealth – he has exaggerated them. The Valenciennes painter was too refined not to be influenced by the affectation which was the fashion of the day: of this we will see more tangible examples further on. This mannerism accounts for the slightly too-sorrowful mourners and the slightly too-perfect landscape. Nevertheless, this picture – and what miniature deserves more to be called a picture! – bears comparison with the best panel paintings. Marmion seems to have become more confident in using the rich palette he had already demonstrated. He employs fewer of the softer hues; his landscape, instead of being blurred on the horizon, preserves its sharp lines and bold tints, and the whole painting is resplendent with color.

A few of the initials decorating the second half of the Pontifical were also painted by Simon Marmion. Those in the first part had been executed around 1400; the liturgical book destined for a bishop of Sens Cathedral was still incomplete. We know nothing of the history of the manuscript after that. It is believed to have come into the hands of another bishop, since only a bishop could possibly have been interested in a book of ritual of that kind. And within the States of Burgundy, William Fillastre seems to be the cleric most likely to have received this charge at that time; he succeeded Jean Chevrot to the episcopal throne of Tournai. Fillastre was also the Abbot of the Benedictine Abbey of St. Bertin, for which Marmion had once worked; the Valenciennes master, having been his protégé, was undoubtedly selected to complete the Pontifical. Earlier, Marmion had painted his patron's portrait in a copy of the *Chroniques de France* destined for Philip the Good. This manuscript, which might be compared to *La Fleur des Histoires* (plates 33 & 34), is preserved in the Hermitage Museum in Leningrad. All these works confirm the opinion expressed by Jean Le Maire when he declared Simon Marmion "the prince of illuminators."

## 39 St. Waudru Arriving in Hibernia

JACQUES DE GUISE, Chroniques de Hainaut, *translated by Jean Wauquelin, Vol. II. Written in Mons, 1449. Decorated in Bruges, between 1455 and 1468.*
*298 folios ($17^1/_4 \times 12^1/_4$"); 69 large miniatures.*
*Ms. 9243, f. 115*

TO UNDERSTAND the illustration of books of history, or of books with historical pretentions like so many of those written during the reign of Philip the Good, it is nearly always necessary also to read the text. We have encountered a few examples of illustrations that show in a single picture a series of different episodes pertaining to the same subject (plates 33 & 34). Here the scene is limited to a single event; nevertheless, in spite of its apparent simplicity, this miniature also requires enlightenment from its literary context.

A certain Maldegar, from the illustrious lineage of Gascony, and his wife of the royal house of France, begot a son whom they called Maldegar, like his father, and who was brought up with great affection. When he had reached the required age and maturity, his parents sent the boy to King Dagobert's court *afin que il peuist atteindre le hault bien de proesce et de chevalerie* (in order that he might attain the fame of high deeds and chivalry). Dagobert became fond of Maldegar and, to show his appreciation, soon made him a knight; he himself girded Maldegar with the sword. The parents, rejoicing at their son's promising start in life, thought of marrying him *à son honneur* and decided that Waudru, the daughter of Waubert, duke of Lotharingia, would make a most suitable bride. The young knight was not willing at first, for he wished to remain *vierge et chaste;* nevertheless, complying with the necessity of continuing the lineage

and of caring for vast domains, he finally yielded. The wedding took place amid the rejoicing of the whole court. Dagobert, to honor this important alliance, offered the islands and country of Hibernia to Maldegar, to be ruled in his name. The young husband hastened to obey the king but had to leave his wife; he carried out his duties with competence and justice, and won "the great joy and obedience" of his people in Ireland. Meanwhile, "my lady St. Waudru, his wife, began to feel very sad for she loved her husband dearly," and she decided to join him. Her landing in Ireland is represented in this miniature. They returned to France and withdrew to their estates, lived very piously, and begot many children. Later, with St. Waudru's assent, Maldegar resolved to give away his properties, and retired to the Abbey of Aumont. As a monk he seems to have taken the name of Vincent, for at this turn in the narrative the author no longer uses the name of Maldegar, but only that of "My lord Saint Vincent." Near the end of his life he founded the Abbey of Soignies, where he died after having worked several miracles.

A life so eventful would have inspired the Master of Mansel or Simon Marmion to compose an entire panorama; the author of this miniature has contented himself with the meeting of the two saints, husband and wife, in imaginary surroundings. The difference does not lie merely in the conception of the illustration; other aspects, especially the aesthetic, are even better evidence of the gap between the two styles of illumination. Waudru's arrival gives the painter the opportunity to gather many people into the picture: the saint's fellow-travelers, and the members of the household and her husband's associates in Ireland who have come to greet her. The men's and women's faces are all alike, only attitudes and coloring bringing a little variety into the picture: a minimum of alternated gestures, some quite unlifelike, and several very hard colors, repeated on different parts of the garments without variation of tone.

The whole process is simple and yet extraordinarily persuasive! The same applies to the setting. The walls are red, blue, and gray, the boulders are unrealistically round, their exaggerated overhang artificially shaded with a golden glaze; the sea is rough, its surface made of stiff regular waves. And yet all this gives the page its naïve charm. The miniaturist, however, was not accustomed to working out his landscape as he was obliged to here. In his other works he seems to have avoided painting nature or, if this was not possible, to have drawn it very summarily. But here he has enjoyed doing it: he has made the meandering Irish coast as complicated as possible, crowding the islands with monasteries, churches, and fortresses by the dozen. Depth is conceived on two planes: the vision is perpendicular from the foreground to beyond the ship, as in a tapestry, but in the upper plane the perspective extends far into the distance.

An archive document allows us to connect a name with this particular style: that of William Vrelant. We read in the records that in 1468, Charles the Bold had paid seventy-two pounds to

William Vrelant for miniatures *de plusieurs couleurs* (in several colors) that he painted for the second volume of the *Chroniques de Hainaut*. Vrelant was a Dutchman, probably from Vrelant, near Utrecht, for he first worked in this episcopal town; he was one of the main exponents of this rather secondary current of Dutch illumination which preferred the harshly modeled linear style to a technique more pictorial and realistic. Having settled in Bruges in 1455, perhaps even earlier, he was the first miniaturist in this town to work according to the new style of illustration, which had already been in use in the southern Netherlands since about 1445. His production was abundant, as he enjoyed the help of many collaborators. The influence of his style is to be found in England and even more in Spain. How to explain that this miniaturist from Bruges took a leading part in the decoration of a work created in Mons, the first volume of which was completed in this town in 1448 and illustrated in an entirely different spirit? A few historical notes help to unravel this puzzle. The translation of Jacques de Guise's work was made by Jean Wauquelin; its first volume was copied in 1448 and decorated shortly after (plate 27). The writing of the second volume was finished in 1449 by Jacotin Du Bois, one of Wauquelin's clerks, who signed his work. It is from this second volume that the present miniature is taken. The third volume was written in 1453, after Wauquelin's death, when his widow was trying to carry on the business. Unfortunately, the second and third volumes had not yet been illustrated. When, in 1455, the *Chroniques de Hainaut* in three parts were deposited in the "Library of Burgundy," the two last were still without decoration. Their miniatures were added later, as, in 1468, Charles the Bold made a payment to Vrelant for the illustration of the second volume and to Loyset Liédet for the third. Philip the Good had probably ordered these volumes to be completed and his son had to pay the bill. The analysis of the decorative techniques reveals this double craftmanship in Bruges and Mons. This shows the fundamental importance of a thorough archaeological examination of the manuscripts, which would make it possible for us to reconstruct the history of illumination even in the absence of historical documents.

40

# Philip the Good Attending a Mass Sung by the Choir of Burgundy

TRAITÉ SUR L'ORAISON DOMINICALE, *translated by Jean Miélot. Perhaps Lille. After 1457.*
*270 folios (15 3/4 × 11 3/4"); 3 large miniatures with marginal decorations.*
*Ms. 9092, f. 9*

SCENES FROM PRIVATE LIFE are rare among the illustrations in the luxurious copies made for the personal use of the Duke of Burgundy. Except for a few book paintings that show Philip the Good paying a visit to David Aubert, his favorite publisher, the duke is usually represented in full dress on the occasion of some formal reception. The miniature decorating the first page of this *Commentary on the Lord's Prayer* is therefore all the more precious since it brings us a less known and probably quite genuine aspect of the duke's life.

We see Philip the Good attending Mass in his private chapel; he kneels under a baldachin and wears the necklace of the Golden Fleece. The choir of the chapel has been isolated by long red curtains hanging from the capitals. Through the arches of the colonnade we can see the windows and the vaults of the ambulatory; the latter could remain open, when necessary, to house larger numbers of attendants at more important religious ceremonies. Within the choir, a private oratory has been arranged for the duke in a structure hung with blue, its border showing at regular intervals the Burgundian insignia. The prince, kneeling on a cushion, is half-turned toward the altar while holding open a prayer book that is lying on a kind of prie-dieu in front of him. The artist has very cleverly arranged this attitude to show the duke at once absorbed in his book and in the ceremony. The first words of the *Pater Noster* are

embroidered in golden thread on the curtain around a small picture made of two jointed panels. On the left panel, a Madonna and Child are distinctly visible, and on the right is seen a kneeling figure dressed in black, certainly the Duke of Burgundy himself. This kind of portable picture was used to accompany its owner when he traveled; the National Library in Vienna has preserved a similar diptych which was carried by Charles the Bold.

The altar is decorated with a brass reredos, probably gilded, presenting three scenes of the Passion: Christ carrying the Cross, the Crucifixion, and the Descent from the Cross. There is only one candelabrum on the altar; in its center is a tall lighted candle, with four smaller ones around the supporting disk. This detail is too particular not to have been drawn from life; the five flames are probably symbolical of the five wounds of Christ. The lighted candle has a liturgical meaning: the real presence of Christ, from the Consecration to Communion, during the Mass. The rug before the altar is beautifully woven with the duke's coat of arms; in other miniatures this carpet is usually spread on Philip the Good's prie-dieu. On the right-hand side of the miniature stands an informal group of singers around a lectern bearing a music manuscript in which the illuminator took the trouble to write down some notes. These chanters must show us the members of the famous choir of the Chapelle de Bourgogne. A few noblemen of the duke's household, one of whom wears the order of the Golden Fleece, are also attending the Mass, standing behind their master's oratory.

The novelty of the subject accounts at least partially for the lively character of the picture. It is further enhanced by the realistic bearing of Philip the Good, by the variety of the countenances and attitudes of the singers, and by the servant dutifully drawing aside the curtain and the acolyte piously performing his duties. It is above all the amazing individuality of the faces which gives a warm human feeling to this already very animated scene.

The artist excels in the art of painting human beings, but he is less able to reproduce the architectural surroundings; he has been unable, for instance, to give a circular shape to the choir behind the altar, nor has he been more successful with the aisles. Moreover, he has set the altar on the axis of the tile flooring, but has failed to do the same with the altar step. Like several other miniaturists (plates 36 & 37), he has enframed the field of vision: the scene is supposed to be seen from between two columns of the ambulatory which the painter wanted to show in his picture. In so doing he increases the difficulty of finding the right perspective, for the latter is bound to be wrong in some details, such as in the tile flooring. These shortcomings, however, do not spoil the general effect of the entire miniature in which a degree of reality prevails that is very rare for the time.

The picture we have just described appears at the beginning of the *Commentary on the Lord's Prayer*. This work was written by an unknown Benedictine monk who is represented in a large miniature at the head of the prologue. Jean Miélot translated the text in 1457, when he was canon of St. Peter's church in Lille; a miniature depicting the presentation of the manuscript to the Duke of Burgundy is painted at the head of his preface. On the basis of this information, this copy has generally been considered to have also been made in Lille in 1457. But this is not yet proven. The luxurious quality of this copy of the book has no counterpart in Miélot's current production. The manuscripts executed in Lille are, besides, usually written on paper, as we shall see in another example (plate 43). Moreover, they never show, as this manuscript does, such richly decorated margins, nor such a number of shields bearing Philip the Good's coat of arms. It is possible however that Miélot wanted to have a really luxurious book to present to his master. Further research on the history of the medieval book will probably give an answer to this problem. For the moment, we must be content to say that this copy was executed between 1457, the date of its translation, and 1467, when the presence of the manuscript in the "Library of Burgundy" is officially attested.

The three miniatures in this splendid manuscript have also been ascribed to Jean Le Tavernier (plates 28, 29, 30, 32, and 36). If this were proved, we could credit the Audenarde miniaturist with still another kind of style and technique in his art. That the picture reproduced here has the liveliness we admire in Jean Le Tavernier's work is undeniable; but is this a valid criterion? This painter, as we know from the archives, had between 1454 and 1460 (plate 36) marvelously developed his grisaille technique. We believe that he also previously adopted, after 1451, a specific watercolor style of which we have a beautiful example on plate 28. He seems to have continued this style up to 1455 (plate 32). But the technique of painting in this *Oraison dominicale* is totally different from those two others (plates 28 & 32). Could it be that Jean Le Tavernier adopted finally the gouache technique of his contemporaries? We would be quite willing to accept this suggestion were it not that the second miniature of the present treatise, which represents a Benedictine monk writing at his desk, is ugly in comparison with the painting in 1455 of the same subject (plate 32). There is too wide a gap in the quality of the two pictures; Jean Le Tavernier, alleged author of the earlier painting, could not possibly have painted a few years later such a poor "remake" of the same subject – what is worse, in a luxury copy destined for Philip the Good. It is simpler, and preferable from the point of view of method, tentatively to ascribe these miniatures to some pupil of Jean Le Tavernier. We know that the master had assistants to whom, in exchange for their help, he taught his craft. When, after a probation period, the apprentice started working on his own, he remained more or less impregnated with the style of his former master, to a measure that varied according to his own gifts and temperament. Only a closer scrutiny of the whole production of the same group would allow one to trace the different artists painting in this same style.

41

# David Aubert Presenting a Copy of *Cy nous dit* to Philip the Good

COMPOSITION DE LA SAINTE ECRITURE or CY NOUS DIT. *Brussels. 1462. 166 folios (16 × 11 3/4"); 16 miniatures in two different shades of grisaille. Ms. 9017, f. 38 v*

MOST OF THE LUXURY copies intended for Philip the Good include a so-called presentation miniature. The offering of books to lay or ecclesiastical dignitaries has been represented in manuscripts since a very early date. At the beginning of the Gothic period, the portraits of the owners of these books were comparatively small. They were usually represented kneeling before God, the Virgin, or certain saints, and the donors had to be painted on a smaller scale than the Divinity or the sacred personages. Such modest portraits would hardly have flattered Jean de Berry's vanity; he was thus the first at the court of France to be represented on a relatively large scale (plate 19). This was the beginning of a fashion in presentation miniatures which reached its peak thirty years later with Philip the Good; of these the most magnificent example preserved is in the *Chroniques de Hainaut* (plate 27).

Historians often interpret the numerous variations of this theme, the presentation of a manuscript, as being inspired, or even copied, from this perfect specimen. Such an explanation is, unfortunately, a trifle too easy. The manuscripts, once completed and handed over to the library of the dukes of Burgundy, certainly became unavailable to the illuminators, for even the best painters were then considered mere artisans. On the other hand, the preparatory sketches, although undoubtedly kept in current use, did not circulate from town to town, but remained

## 42 The Emperor Anthony Victorious over the Saracens

JEAN WAUQUELIN, L'histoire de Sainte Hélène. *Bruges. Before 1467.*
*180 folios ($14^1/_2 \times 10^7/_8$"); 26 miniatures.*
*Ms. 9967, f. 18*

WHO WOULD BELIEVE that the life of St. Helen, the mother of St. Martin of Tours, could possibly have inspired such a sanguinary and violent illustration? The medieval chroniclers did not hesitate to introduce into their works the most extraordinary legends to satisfy their thirst for the miraculous. The story of St. Helen is one of these fantastic adventures. The miniature shown from this book is one of the numerous battle scenes painted in the manuscript; it has, however, the distinction of being one of the best pages by Loyset Liédet, the most popular miniaturist of the court of Burgundy.

Anthony, legendary Emperor of Constantinople, is here defending Rome against the Saracens; he has been fighting outside the walls of the holy city which has been spared from the infidels thanks to his bravery. As a token of special gratitude Anthony was given the Roman Emperor's daughter in marriage. Some time after, the new empress gave birth to a lovely daughter who was called Helen. Her birth unfortunately caused her mother's death. The bereaved husband fell in love with his own daughter and was granted leave by the Pope to marry her, on the condition that he would defend Rome against the Moors. The maiden succeeded in escaping secretly and, after many adventures, she eventually landed in England where she married King Henry. She gave birth to several children, one of whom became St. Martin of Tours. She had many friends and

Quant ce vinst au .iij. iour et que lempereur
Anthoine vist que ses gens estoient rafreschis
il fist crier a son de trompe que ses gens dar
mes fussent prestz et armez car il vouloit combatre ace

also a few enemies. Among the latter was her mother-in-law, who was not of the mildest temperament. Anthony, however, did not give up the pursuit of his daughter and poor Helen had to wander over Europe in disguise to escape this incestuous love. One day, her father and her husband met and reached an agreement of some kind, the children welcomed back their mother, and the whole family returned to Rome. As can be expected, all ended well and the author, whose imagination had run dry, it seems, let the parents die shortly after their return to the holy city.

The miniaturist does not follow the text too closely. The town here is anything but Rome. As for the battle, it is like many others found in illuminated manuscripts. We must be grateful to the painter for not forgetting to put turbans on the heads of the defeated enemy as a reminder that the victory was certainly won against the Saracens. This loose interpretation of the text is typical of Loyset Liédet's manner. We can easily imagine him reading the heading of the chapter, of course quite brief and written in rubric, and starting to sketch straightway a very simple scene which he crowds as usual with many people. What a contrast with the Master of Mansel or Simon Marmion, who felt bound to read the whole chapter before selecting its main episodes and including them in a very well-balanced composition! For Loyset Liédet, the first sketch never takes very long nor is it too perfected, for he loves colors and is always eager to take up his palette. When he makes up his mind to concern himself with his work he can do something really charming, with warm and lively hues. The coloring is the criterion by which we can easily distinguish Liédet's work from that of his numerous assistants; their palette is often the same as their master's, but it is never quite so brilliant and they do not succeed in matching the shades as well as he does.

We have no proof other than that of style for ascribing this page and the others found in this manuscript to Loyset Liédet. His work is so characteristic that there is no chance of our being mistaken, at least where works of such quality are concerned. We know his hand well, thanks to the miniatures in several manuscripts which are definitely ascribed to him, among them the third volume of the *Chroniques de Hainaut*, already quoted with regard to the collaboration of William Vrelant in its second volume (plate 39). We find in this third volume the same kind of illustration: a single subject, faithfully rendered and in no way exaggerated. In this respect his work is similar to that of his colleague and rival in Bruges, William Vrelant.

This copy for Philip the Good of the story of St. Helen is absolutely typical of the kind of book issuing from David Aubert's workshop during the time he worked in Bruges. Born in Hesdin, in Artois, Aubert was the greatest of all publishers of texts during the reign of the *Grand Duc d'Occident*. We have seen that he worked with Jean Le Tavernier, the specialist in grisaille, to produce jointly, at some time before 1460, the three volumes of the *Chroniques et Conquêtes de Charlemagne* (plate 36). In 1462, when established in Brussels, or perhaps just passing through, Aubert presented Philip the Good with a magnificent copy of the *Composition de la Sainte Ecriture* (plate 41) which was probably illuminated by Dreux Jean. Soon after this, he came to Bruges where he published numerous texts, making many precious copies in his own hand, among which is the *Histoire de Sainte Hélène*. While there, he tried to impose the fashion of publishing books without marginal decorations. In this milieu, where bourgeois patronage was expanding every day, David Aubert adopted a spectacularly large format for his books, one work comprising in some instances four, five, or even ten volumes, but they were not of a very refined presentation. He worked in this town with his fellow citizen, Loyset Liédet, who represented him more than once in his pictures, particularly on the occasion of the duke's visits to his publisher.

The archives, unfortunately, are rarely of much help in reconstructing the life of medieval artists, and it is usually risky to try to identify an artist's hand when he was still a mere assistant in a large atelier. It is perhaps possible, however, to recognize Loyset Liédet because he always drew his figures with a harsh outline, thus accentuating the bony structure of their faces. It is probable that he had learned his craft in Jean Wauquelin's workshop in Mons, where he may even have helped in the illuminating of the first volume of the *Chroniques de Hainaut*. Later on, he certainly worked under Simon Marmion, for around 1454, when he was on his own in Hesdin, he still painted in the manner of the Valenciennes master, adopting even the latter's kind of composition for various subjects and his soft colors. Once in Bruges, where he may have arrived before David Aubert, Liédet changed this elaborate manner into something plainer, more adapted to the simpler tastes of the new milieu in which he was living. No Flemish illuminator has ever shown so many discrepancies in the quality of his production; no one seems either to have produced so much. Judging from the number of his manuscripts preserved in the "Library of Burgundy," one might easily believe that he was Philip the Good's favorite illuminator. No other book illumination is so marked with the mannerism of its time: Loyset Liédet is the Dirk Bouts of miniature painting.

# 43 Two Episodes from the *Romance of Girart of Nevers*

ROMANCE DE GIRART DE NEVERS. *Probably Lille. Before 1466.*
*126 paper folios (11³/₈ × 6"); 54 pen drawings with color wash.*
*Ms. 9631, ff. 77 and 26 v*

FOR SOME AESTHETIC REASON, these two miniatures in the *Romance of Girart of Nevers* are not inserted according to the pagination nor the chronological order of the narrative. One might wonder why these simple sketches were chosen to be included in the present volume. This technique of illustration, although undeniably modest, is not quite as simple as it first appears; it reveals, moreover, an artistic comprehension that was rarely to be found during the Middle Ages. Apart from that, this style of illumination gives us an opportunity to become acquainted with a kind of text and a category of books of which no mention has so far been made here: the romance of chivalry.

In 1110, says the writer, King Louis the Fat held a great party in his palace. Girart, count of Nevers, the handsomest, bravest, and noblest knight at the whole court, sang in praise of his sweetheart, Euryant, *la plus belle*, *la plus courtoise*, *la plus humble de France*, whom he loved and who loved him too. He even went to the point of challenging anyone who would venture to question her loyalty. Liziart, count of Forest, accepted the challenge and made the wager that he would have Euryant *à tout son vouloir sans en avoir refus* (at his will with no denial), pledging his estates if he failed. But Euryant was true to her love. Liziart had already lost hope when the damsel's maid, hearing of the count's designs, decided she would help him, and

betrayed her mistress. Liziart was invited to look through a hole in the wall to see a mark resembling a violet on *la dextre mamelle* (the right breast) of the beautiful Euryant. The Count of Forest rode back to the court and, on the strength of this very intimate information, won his wager to the great chagrin of Girart and Euryant. One can easily guess that the two lovers went through many an adventure before virtue and beauty could triumph again. Girart drove Euryant out, after having first thought of killing her. Later on he learned of Liziart's villainy, brought back his sweetheart, and publicly confounded the felon. He thus became Count of Forest as well as Nevers, and *prist a maryage Euryant sa mie* (took Euryant as his wife).

The two miniatures describe two happy events in the long series of misfortunes that befell the separated lovers. In the first one, below, Girart has become a minstrel. Deprived of his estates by the schemes of Liziart, he learned the art of juggling from a master of that craft. Under the disguise of his new profession, he came to the Count of Forest's manor and sang before him, *la vyole pendue a son col* (with his viol hanging from his neck). After his recital, as he was sitting by the open fire, he heard Euryant's maid – who in the meantime had become Liziart's mistress – remind the Count of Forest of how much he was indebted to her for his present wealth, and he recounting all the details of her treachery. Liziart at that time admits that he had never succeeded in seducing Euryant. In the face of such revelations Girart could hardly conceal his emotions; he left the castle at the first opportunity and started his campaign for the recovery of his rights and his "belle."

The second miniature concerns a story which is prettier still. Following heroic battles fought before Cologne, Girart was invited to the court of the Duke of Milon. There he was given a carefully brewed philtre to drink which made him fall in love with Aiglantine and desire to marry her. One fine morning, her hawk on his arm, he went out with his equerry to ride in the woods. He was full of joy and singing in a loud voice in the hope that the wind would carry his song to his new love. Turning around, he saw her looking at him from one of the castle windows. He was already dreaming of their love when a lark alighted singing, just in front of him. The hawk pulled on its lead and tried to escape; once freed, it dashed at the poor bird that was flying away and brought it back dead to its master. Looking at the bird in his hand Girart saw that it carried Euryant's ring around its neck. Dumfounded, he resolved to atone for his betrayal of his true love and sent the equerry straightway to Aiglantine with orders to give her back the hawk.

To "turn into prose" a chivalric romance in verse offered, like all literature of its kind, a rich and inexhaustible opportunity to an imaginative illustrator. The conventional style of miniature painting was possibly too rich and heavy for such a fanciful literary genre. On the other hand, pen drawing, at the same time picturesque and simpler, was very suitable.

Several manuscripts written on paper like this one and containing similar romances decorated with the same type of illumination had been written for Jean de Wavrin, who was a book connoisseur, a gentleman at arms, and the author of the *Anciennes Chroniques d'Angleterre*. This miniaturist therefore has been styled the Master of Wavrin, and he certainly was an unrivalled draftsman of the Burgundian period.

We know enough about medieval books made during the reign of Philip the Good to allow us to say that close to a dozen manuscripts, all romances of chivalry written on paper and decorated with color-washed pen drawings, came from a workshop established in Lille. This atelier followed a well-known Lille tradition. Jean Miélot, a publisher established in this town from 1455 onward, had been bringing out many works, generally written on paper and also decorated with pen drawings or a kind of watercolor (plate 32). The city of Lille must have been saturated with works of spirituality, in which the monks of the Church of St. Peter were specialists. His rival launched a new type of book: the romance of chivalry, inspired by its older, longer prototype in verse, which he turned into prose. This less highbrow but more exciting publisher was fortunate enough to meet this first-rate draftsman, the so-called Master of Wavrin. The miniature painters of these glorious days did their best to evoke, by means of the most gorgeous and refined techniques, the glamour of life – movements, colors, feelings – and sometimes even several of these aspects of the real world at once. But the Master of Wavrin goes well beyond this experimental stage; he succeeds in extracting from an episode, the fact most worthy of notice. He is engrossed in the essential while remaining aloof from the complexity of the subject, and with a deft pen and firm strokes catches without hesitation the essence of the scene. In this sense he is a caricaturist, but he is more than that, for even his surprisingly restricted sketches always include a detail which increases their gusto, such as the two dogs in front of the table, the other dog waiting anxiously to catch its prey, or the two horses in the shade of the trees, both delightful little additions. Nobody knows whether the Master of Wavrin was appreciated in his time. He had no illustrious patron since his art was probably too sober, his means too simple. He was obliged to share the illustration of manuscripts with pale imitators. Unfortunately, one cannot imitate such a subtle art: the result, if it is not a masterpiece, is a deplorable failure. The Master of Wavrin was probably not understood because he was ahead of his time. In all the history of Flemish illumination, no artist has shown himself closer to us in his technique and in his vision of the world.

# 44 The Entry into Jerusalem

LA PASSION DE NOTRE SEIGNEUR, *possibly translated by Jean Mansel, with two sermons of Jean Gerson on the same sheet. Probably Brussels. Before 1467.*
*218 folios ($16^1/_8 \times 9^1/_2$"); 7 historiated initials; 7 half-page miniatures.*
*Ms. 9081–82, f. 5*

TO THE ICONOGRAPHY of the Entry into Jerusalem, this miniature offers a very original variation: the procession marches from right to left, while normally the town is on the right side, and approached from the left of the picture. This change in a much-used theme is presumably made from the desire for originality. The illuminator is also at variance with traditional representations in endeavoring to enliven his painting by giving real individuality to certain characters in Christ's retinue. The illustration of the Passion generally begins with the triumphant entry into Jerusalem, but the inhabitants of the town usually express their enthusiastic welcome by waving palms and throwing their mantles on the ground; in this miniature, however, the interest of the onlookers is shown in only a few of their attitudes and gestures. Among the people who welcome Christ at the gate of the town is a man who respectfully takes off his hat, while his neighbor, leaning on his shoulder and pressing his arm, presumably inquires about the newcomer's identity; another character hurriedly removes his mantle to spread it in front of the donkey carrying the Messiah. The heads of a few of the disciples have fine golden circles, since a large gold halo was apparently not to the artist's taste. We notice in the group Peter's massive form and bearded face, and the Apostle John's youthful stance and smooth cheek. They seem quite surprised at the cordial welcome bestowed on their Master.

Behind Christ, in the center of the picture, is a tree with a boy perched in its branches. This detail is retained from earlier representations where it is easily understood: children have climbed into a tree either to cut palms for throwing at the feet of the Master, or simply in order to see Christ over the top of the crowd. As one can see, neither of these motives applies in this miniature; it seems rather that the boy looks toward the two children who wave palms on the balcony over the gate.

This representation of Christ's entry into Jerusalem has a very classical composition. In the middle are Christ and the child in the tree, isolated from the group of men on both sides; behind them on the left is the gate of the town, the towering hills on the right. The city walls beyond the gate extend into the landscape. The impression of depth is conveyed by a succession of overlapping planes rather than by the meandering road which generally links the fore- and backgrounds of miniatures and paintings in the fifteenth century.

The miniaturist has made use of a *grisaille à la gouache* handled in the same manner as in the *Composition de la Sainte Ecriture* (plate 41) and with perhaps even more refinement. Here, however, the painter did not limit his palette to black and white with a slight gold glaze, but added a very light touch of blue which makes the figures and the gate of the town in the foreground contrast admirably with the landscape. He has also added faint shades of red to the faces. This is enough to give the picture a quite different appearance from that of the frontispiece folio of the *Composition de la Sainte Ecriture*. The miniature here is less harsh, for it has lost the metallic brightness so noticeable in the production of Jean Le Tavernier (plate 36) and Dreux Jean, though it was already less apparent in the latter's work. Its softness also comes from the pictorial technique itself: the painting is more gentle, the brushwork is lighter and more delicate. The two frontispieces, in the *Composition de la Sainte Ecriture* (plate 41) and *La Passion de Notre Seigneur* (plate 44), are nevertheless too similar for us not to think of the same painter. In both is used the same grisaille and a human type with individual features and lively eyes, as well as a particularly deep perspective. In the second miniature, though, the master gives proof of a surer and more refined talent. If Dreux Jean painted the first miniature of the other manuscript, then he is also the author of this one. A certain detail in the decoration of this book adds weight to the identification we are here suggesting. The frontispiece folio of *La Passion de Notre Seigneur* is surrounded by a gold frame enclosing the first folio of the *Composition de la Sainte Ecriture*. We will soon have a chance to note the persistence of this technical detail in the same workshop; one so seldom encounters it in the history of illumination and book decoration that its presence here is unexpectedly conclusive.

That the miniatures were painted by an illuminator who lived in Brussels in 1462 is no proof that the manuscript was made there and at that time, even though the *Composition de la*

*Sainte Ecriture* was dated and localized in that town. Fortunately, secondary decorations appear in this manuscript which differ from those of the well-known workshops of Bruges, Ghent, Mons, Lille, or Valenciennes, and they do resemble those in some of the manuscripts made in Brussels. The script, besides, is definitely in David Aubert's style. Is it by his own hand, *manu propria* as he often states, or by the hand of one of his apprentices? He worked in Brussels in 1472; did he write this manuscript before he settled in Bruges? In this case, the copy of *La Passion de Notre Seigneur* would have been made only shortly after the *Composition de la Sainte Ecriture.* If the script is the work of an assistant established in Brussels, we can push back its date as far as 1467, but no earlier, for the manuscript appears in the inventory made during that year, after the death of Philip the Good. We cannot, for the moment, solve this problem of date; in any case, a miniature of such quality unquestionably attests the great originality displayed in the production of luxurious books in Brussels during the reign of the Grand Duke of the Occident.

45

# Margaret of York at Prayer

COLLECTION OF SEVERAL SPIRITUAL TREATISES. *Ghent. Between 1467 and 1477.*
*307 folios (15 1/8 × 10 7/8"); 5 miniatures with marginal decorations.*
*Ms. 9272–76, f. 182*

THE POLITICAL UNIFICATION of the States grouped under the sovereignty of Philip the Good was a slow process, in spite of the duke's high diplomatic and military successes. Slow, too, was the development of a common style in the domain of art. During the reign of the Grand Duke an impressive number of talented miniaturists appear after 1445, but they are scattered in various areas and display very dissimilar styles. The first among them to impose a new style by the superiority of their production are the illustrators of an important group of manuscripts coming from the workshop of Jean Wauquelin in Mons; the best book paintings are those ascribed to Simon Marmion. He established himself in 1458 in Valenciennes after having worked in Amiens and in other towns in northern France. There are many other miniaturists whose originality we have admired in the previous plates (plates 26 to 36, and 38 to 43); they have each their vision of man and man's everyday surroundings, which they paint in their individual ways. It is too early to call this a style, strictly speaking; it is rather that several styles are meeting and influencing each other. Under Charles the Bold uniformity is more apparent, but at that time the production of painted books had moved from south to north, along an axis passing through Bruges, Ghent, and Brussels, while the southern Netherlands had become entirely unproductive.

C.xxiiij

Orison sur la premiere partie de la patenostre auec la premiere demande. Pater nr̃e et c̃.

Vous auez voulu sire tout puissant que en nostre priere nous nommons vous et apellons nr̃e pere Or soit je vous suplie ce nom sanctifie et conferme

This portrait of a lady kneeling at prayer is an excellent example of the quality to be seen in the illustration of manuscripts during this new period of Flemish illumination. The page is not exceptional; it is not even a frontispiece. At the time of Philip the Good's patronage, an illumination like this – a portrait, or at least a copy of a portrait – would certainly have been placed at the head of the manuscript and not at the end, as it is here. This fact alone is evidence of a subtle but undeniable loosening of the concept of decoration, and we shall see that the artists also become freer in their expression of aesthetic values.

The subject of the miniature needs no commentary: a lady is praying before the Holy Trinity. It is easy to identify her: she is Margaret of York, wife of Charles the Bold. We also find her in a manuscript preserved in the Convent of the Poor Clares in Ghent, where she is painted at the Duke of Burgundy's side, and in several other manuscripts that were made for her personally, as well as in a panel painting belonging to the Lehman Collection in New York. This collection of moral treatises and prayers was executed for Margaret, the sister of Edward IV of England; she did not sign this manuscript, as was her custom (plate 46), but her coat of arms is painted in the margin of the frontispiece folio. Other manuscripts (plate 46) with similar contents vouch for this princess' genuine interest in the spiritual life.

The Trinity on the altar shows a most original conception. The Father is seated holding a Christ of Sorrows in His arms in the manner of a pietà. Our miniature differs on this point from the *Trinity* in Frankfurt by the Master of Flémalle, where the Father holds His Son beneath the arms to prevent His collapse. The two pictures are nevertheless inspired by the same iconography of the Three Persons, in which the Son is painted not in glory, following His Resurrection, but still marked with the wounds and suffering of the Passion. In the miniature the Holy Ghost, in the form of a dove, flies down to Jesus, its beak pointing toward His head symbolizing the spiritual collaboration in the work of the Redemption. Another detail, also absent from the Frankfurt painting: Christ's feet rest on a globe, the symbol of the world redeemed through His sufferings.

The group of the Three Divine Persons does not rest on a socle but merely on top of the altar; therefore it is not meant to represent a statue but rather to suggest what the kneeling figure has in mind as she addresses her prayer to the Holy Trinity. A closed altarpiece is behind it; it is decorated with paintings or statues which, as far as we can see, represent St. Peter and St. Paul. The miniaturist, rather audaciously, does not show the whole altarpiece, but only part of the two saints, visible to shoulder height. Cut off in the same way, only the lower part of the window appears in the miniature. The artist did not feel bound to frame his subject with architectural motifs, such as walls and columns (plates 36, 37, and 40), nor did he consider it necessary to paint in a well-defined background (plate 44). He has simply created the space necessary for his figures. It is in this sense also that the artist may be considered more free; he is no longer a slave to the conventional compositions and standard backgrounds of the preceding period.

The use of grisaille, as we have already seen (plate 44), had awakened the miniaturists' sensitivity to the charm of soft shades. Around 1470, works in grisaille were gradually and discreetly adorned with colors blending well with this process. Such paintings are found in a number of manuscripts, and in several cases their colophons state that they were executed in Ghent. The process is usually accompanied by a special marginal decoration of blue and grayish-gold acanthus leaves, which is a technique typical of this atelier. This technique, as well as the particular style of the painting to be found in the page represented here, are both characteristic of a workshop localized in Ghent that will later play an essential part in the history of Flemish miniatures. Margaret of York placed orders for several books from this atelier, some of which are very luxurious. Such high patronage is without doubt the reason for the increasing quality noticeable in this group of manuscripts before 1477 when Charles the Bold died.

# 46 Margaret of York Practicing the Seven Acts of Mercy

BENOIS SERONT LES MISÉRICORDIEUX, *translated by Nicolas Finet.*
*Brussels. Between 1468 and 1477.*
*213 folios (14$^{5}/_{8}$ × 10$^{1}/_{2}$"); 2 miniatures with marginal decorations.*
*Ms. 9296, f. 1*

ONE OF THE THREE MINIATURES of the *Commentary on the Lord's Prayer* (plate 40) showed Philip the Good attending Mass in his oratory. The unceremonious character of this illustration was here underlined because it is unexpected in relation to the most powerful prince of Europe of those days. More intimate still was the portrait of Margaret of York in the preceding manuscript: a collection of spiritual works, written and decorated for this princess (plate 45). In the frontispiece of *Benois seront les miséricordieux* (*Blessed are the Merciful*), the Duchess of Burgundy appears in even greater simplicity, performing the Seven Acts of Mercy as though they were ordinary scenes from her daily life.

The picture is divided into two rows of four compartments each: seven scenes are dedicated to the works of mercy, and the eighth shows the princess at prayer. She is kneeling on a prie-dieu covered by a woven cloth ornamented with her coat of arms; behind her is her patron, St. Margaret, standing on a dragon, her attribute. Between the upper and the lower series are lozenges decorated with the initials *C* and *M*, and with the coat of arms of Margaret of York, duchess of Burgundy and princess of England. The four scenes of the top section are painted before a background which is continuous from one compartment to the other: the buildings are not interrupted by the gold frame which surrounds each little picture; whereas in the lower section, the backgrounds have no relation to each other.

The complex of images grouped in this one miniature draws its inspiration from the Gospels. The title of the manuscript is taken directly from the fifth Beatitude in the sermon on the Mount: "Blessed are the merciful: for they shall obtain mercy" (Matt. 5 : 7). Six of the seven works of mercy painted here come from the prophetic speech pronounced by Christ shortly before his Passion: "For I was an hungred, and ye gave me meat: I was thirsty, and ye gave me drink: I was a stranger, and ye took me in: Naked, and ye clothed me: I was sick, and ye visited me: I was in prison, and ye came unto me" (Matt. 25 : 35–36).

The painter has, nevertheless, altered the order of the acts of mercy: the naked are clothed before the stranger is sheltered, the prisoners visited before the sick. When the disciples asked Christ to name the occasion when they had given Him assistance of this sort, the Master replied: "Inasmuch as ye have done it unto one of the least of these my brethren, ye have done it unto me." Christ's presence is indicated in each of the six paintings by His cruciform halo; clad in blue, He stands by the side of the needy to whom the duchess gives assistance. The seventh work of mercy, the burial of the dead, is not cited in the Gospel enumeration and therefore Christ is not present. It would be interesting to know when and where this last work of mercy was added to the other six. Margaret of York does not appear in this seventh compartment, but possibly the last two pictures are linked together; the participation of the duchess in the last work of mercy would thus be manifested in her figure, praying for the deceased. If one does not agree with this interpretation it is hard to understand why the princess seems to be looking toward the seventh scene, rather than praying before an image of the Divinity or of a saint. A link between the two pictures may also be indicated by the raised corner of the curtain. The setting of this page must have been a real problem for the illuminator, but he could hardly have solved it more successfully. The artist has worked out each one of his small pictures as carefully as if they had been separate miniatures; his work is the more meticulous because of their very small size. He was really a great master of composition. In this respect he has been particularly successful with the single scenes, yet he displays an astonishing variety in his presentation of the subjects. His skill is also to be seen in the actions and bearing of his characters. The architectural backgrounds are most minutely rendered, the settings laid out on divergent planes. This artist was sensitive to many aspects of reality, which he painted according to his own formula. The types of faces and special coloring are the main characteristics of his work. The women's faces, sketched with a few minute black strokes, have an air of rare distinction; the men's are more elaborate, showing, with the addition of color, the same expressive features we have already admired in the pictures ascribed to Dreux Jean (plates 41 & 44), and also the same way of painting the eyes and adding a little red dash to the cheek. The refinement that we noticed in *La Passion de Notre*

*Seigneur* (plate 44), which was further enhanced in the *Composition de la Sainte Ecriture* (plate 41), is still more accentuated here. For the first time we see this master relinquishing grisaille to try his hand at colors. He likes bright shades and his taste remains unerring; he has even ventured a daring purple, but his creative talent is to be seen best in the pastel hues of the background buildings. This master has continued to improve the style he displayed in the two earlier works mentioned above. It is to such artists that the Flemish palette owes its enrichment, by his introduction of colors not used therein before.

The attribution to Dreux Jean is here reconfirmed by the gold border he had already employed in the two frontispieces just mentioned. It is in this case an actual frame, for it is painted in perspective, with controlled lights and shadows. Let us repeat, such details considered alone are insufficient to lay the foundation of a hypothesis; they acquire value only when confronted with other concordant facts. But there are in this book some marginal decorations in a style encountered only in the manuscripts executed in Brussels. Moreover, the second miniature of the manuscript presents, in the same hand, Margaret of York in a view of Brussels, with St. Gudula's Collegiate Church, on a large scale, in the very center of the page, and the Church of the Sablon in the background. It becomes difficult to disregard such an accumulation of evidence that all points to the capital of Brabant as the origin of this manuscript. The presence in the initial of the letters *C* and *M*, standing for Charles and Margaret, allows us to fix its execution some time between 1468, the date of their wedding, and 1477, when Charles, duke of Burgundy, died.

47

# Scipio Africanus Sending His Spies to the Numidian Camp

FRONTIN, Livre des Stratagèmes, *translated by Jean de Rovroy. France. 1471.*
*127 folios ($8^{1}/_{4} \times 7^{1}/_{2}''$); 1 large historiated initial; many other initials with human heads; 1 marginal border with putti; 52 miniatures.*
*Ms. 10475, f. 8*

TOWARD THE END of the Middle Ages ancient Greek and Roman history became increasingly popular. From the fifteenth century onward many a classical author was translated and adapted. Medieval historians hastened to select from this wealth of material all that could possibly help the causes which they themselves wished to promote: for instance, the ancient origin of some royal or princely family was made to go back to the Trojans, or a glorious past was found for a country of the new Europe. Jacques de Guise and Jean Wauquelin, when working on the *Chroniques de Hainaut,* often delved into Roman history to find references to the provinces about which they were writing. Frontin's work is a kind of compilation in which the author has assembled tales of the ancient captains who had recourse to stratagems to crush their enemies. In the foreword addressed to Charles VII, king of France, the translator thought it necessary to explain the title of his work: "*Le Livre des Stratagèmes,*" he specifies, "that is to say, the book of the wiles and subtleties employed in deeds of war and chivalry." Since most of the quotations from the classics were too terse to be understood by the people of his time, the translator, very methodically and conscientiously, added comments of his own, carefully headed by the reference "the translator."

Each chapter of the *Livre des Stratagèmes* is preceded by a miniature. The illumination we see

et emmena sauuement sa compaignie sans ce quelle sappar-
ceust. de la cause pourquoy il le faisoit. Metellus pius.

En la guerre despaigne. quant on demanda a metellus
pius quil feroit le lendemain. Il respondit. Se ma robe dist
il le pouoit dire. Je la brulleroie. Marcus licinius crassus.

Au temps de la guerre des fuitifz. quant marcus licini-
crassus fut envoie contre eulx. et ung homme darmes lui dema-
da une foiz. quant il desloigeroit il respondit au demandeur.
As tu paour dist que tu ne oyes la trompette.

Second chappitre des manieres. Comment on peut savoir
le secret des ennemis

here illustrates the text from chapter 2: "How one can learn the enemy's secret." The first example is drawn from Livy's account of the wars of Scipio Africanus. Scipio, during the second African war, had to fight two enemies at once: Hasdrubal, who commanded the Carthaginians, and Sifax, leader of the Numidian battalions. Scipio, taking advantage of the fact that his legate Lelius was going on a mission to Sifax, sent with him certain tribunes and centurions whom he ordered to disguise themselves as valets. Once in the enemy's camp, the valets surreptitiously released one of their horses. They chased it through the camp and thus had the opportunity of noticing that the fortifications were made of piled-up reeds. On the strength of this information, Scipio dispatched Lelius and another officer during the night to set fire to the barricade at opposite ends of the enemy camp. The Numidians, thinking it a mere accident, hurried to extinguish the fires, without bothering to take up their arms. Part of the Roman forces placed them in ambush, and all the Numidians were slaughtered. When the Carthaginians noticed the fires in the allied camp they rushed to help their allies, with no thought of Roman trickery. But Scipio had foreseen the reactions of both his enemies and was waiting, ready to strike with the rest of the Roman forces. The conclusion of this tale is: *qu'il n'en reschappa mie ung pour aller dire aux aultres les nouvelles* (that no one escaped to tell the tale).

Such a subject must have presented many problems to the illuminator. First of all, he was obliged to respect the unity of place; this meant he had to put both tents, Scipio's and Sifax's, in the same picture. Unfortunately, he contented himself with a rather poor contrivance that sets them apart by a sudden shift in the level of the ground on which the camps were built, thus challenging all the laws of perspective. He also endeavored to reproduce in their faces and gestures the actual state of mind of those in each camp. To the left are the Numidians, whose fortified position was near the town they had come to defend. Sifax, wearing a royal crown, is surrounded by his general staff; one can read their great anxiety on their faces, for they know well the military power of their enemy, who had defeated them so often. The tents of the Roman army occupy the right of the picture. Scipio, crowned in the Roman style, instructs the three spies dressed as valets, who are kneeling in front of him. Further back, the legate Lelius is already on his horse, ready to go and deliver his message to the Numidians. The banner on top of one of the Roman tents bears the letters: "*S. R. Q. P.*" The miniaturist has made a mistake in the order of those letters, for he certainly wanted to paint: "*S. P. Q. R.*," for *Senatus Populusque Romanus*, motto of the Latin republic. The other banners have different signs, for instance: *H* (or *M*) and *W* united with a love knot; these are probably the cryptograms that medieval miniaturists, particularly in the fifteenth century, seem to have enjoyed introducing into their paintings; in many cases these are still mysterious to us.

The miniature tells only one part of the story, which is reason enough to assert that the painter was not a brilliant illustrator. His intention was to represent the group of warriors around Scipio and Sifax on a scale sufficiently large for clarity, but he consequently had not room enough to include the defensive camp of the Numidians, a very important element in the story. The landscape, too, does not help us to understand the action: the wonderful town with its accumulation of walls, towers, and useless bridges is nothing but a charming space-filler. Taken separately, the various parts of the painting are naïve and delightfully lifelike, but the general effect is a failure. The genuine aesthetic qualities fortunately make up for the feebleness of the narrative character of this page.

For when he is interpreting action, the painter may be considered to rival Jean Le Tavernier (plate 36): both artists love animated and crowded subjects, and pay great attention to details. His figures are more individualized than those by the miniaturist from Audenarde, and his attitudes are not so rigid. In other ways the art of our painter differs entirely from that of his Flemish colleagues. One cannot find either in miniatures or in paintings of the Netherlands anything comparable to the refinement and depth of this artist's landscapes. The horizon is lost in the imperceptibly graded blue of the skies. His colors also are different; the green, for example, is applied with minute strokes in an enormous range of shades from yellow to blue. The dominant brown used for the rest of the painting and particularly for the faces is unfortunately monotonous, but there is compensation in the lively modeling of the features and the amazing effect of solidity and volume. In many respects the style of this miniature reminds one of Jean Fouquet's work: the same depth and transparency of landscape views, and the choice of darkish colors for the complexions of his characters.

This brilliant pupil of the illustrious painter from Tours is called the Master of the Geneva Boccaccio, the manuscript considered to be his masterpiece. He is in all ways the opposite of his contemporary, Master François, who was the leading exponent of the other trend of French miniature painting, and unfortunately carried the day.

Jean de Rovroy had written his translation in 1461, ten years before our copy was finished. The book is entirely French in technique, from the script, the initials, and the marginal decoration of the frontispiece folio, to the miniatures. Italian influence, however, can be felt in the very classical heads which decorate some initials, as well as in the nude grotesques in the margin. No better example could possibly be found than this French manuscript to show the transition between the preceding Flemish series and the Italian miniature we shall shortly see (plate 49).

# St. Barbara

BOOK OF HOURS OF PHILIP OF CLEVES. *Ghent. Presumably before 1485. 145 folios ($5^1/_8 \times 3^1/_2''$); numerous varied marginal decorations; 24 small miniatures for the calendar; 36 full-page miniatures.*
*Ms. IV 40, ff. 17 v and 18 r*

THIS DOUBLE-PAGE MINIATURE in itself shows the development of another stage in the history of the medieval book. By comparison with the big in-folios of the Burgundian period, this book is diminutive; nevertheless, St. Barbara, the subject of the principal miniature, is painted on a proportionately larger scale than the figures in the much bigger paintings in previous manuscripts. There is another contrast worth noticing between this book and its predecessors in the relationship between the text and the illumination. This is more subtle, and deserves comment at length; we will come back to it later.

It is without doubt St. Barbara who is represented on this double page: the tower with the three lancet windows that the saint holds in her hands is her personal symbol, the various scenes painted in the margin illustrate episodes of her martyrdom, and, finally, these miniatures decorate the first folio of the Hours devoted to her worship. The office in honor of a saint is seldom to be met in medieval books of hours; one usually finds the Hours of Our Lady, of the Cross, of the Passion, or of the Holy Ghost. The devotion to a private saint was generally not manifested except by an anthem or a prayer.

The symbolical tower carried by the saint is an element of the legend of her life: her father Dioscuros, a rich pagan who often traveled great distances, ordered a tower to be built in which he shut up his daughter to shelter her exceptional beauty. Despite her seclusion, Barbara was instructed, allegedly by Origen, in the element of the Christian faith. To her tower, which had but two windows, the maiden is said to have added a third in honor of the Trinity: a detail that the illuminator has not omitted. At his return the father heard of his daughter's conversion and endeavored to bring her back to the worship of Roman gods. The

Incipiunt hore beate barba
Domine la
bia mea
aperies.
Et os me
um ānū
ciabit laudem tuam.
Deus in adiutoriū
meum intende.
Domine ad adiuuandū
me festina
Gloria patri et filio
et spiritui sancto.
Sicut erat in prima
pio et nunc et semper:

49

# The Apostles Peter and Andrew Answering the Call of Christ

MISSAL OF MA[illegible] CORVINUS, KING OF HUNGARY. *Florence. Between 1485 and 1487.*
*431 folios (15 3/4 × 11"); many border decorations with medallions; historiated initials; 2 miniatures; 2 fully decorated double pages facing each other.*
*Ms. 9008, f. 286*

IT IS NOT NECESSARY to make a very thorough examination of this miniature to appreciate the fact that its aesthetic merits are entirely different from those to be seen in the various Flemish pictures reproduced in this volume. Though the page from the *Livre des Stratagèmes* (plate 47) ought to have prepared us for this difference, the gap between the two styles is still surprising. Let us make no mistake; the contrast between both styles, the Flemish and the Italian, lies much more in the artist's vision than in what he sees. Thus, broadly speaking, we can use the term "realism" in connection with both arts, for both of them had in mind to represent "reality." The individual artists, however, each saw the world from a personal angle, strongly marked by his own cultural and aesthetic traditions. This must be borne in mind when analyzing this painting, for it is so astonishing when compared to the great majority of our earlier illuminations.

The subject of this picture is taken from the Gospel of St. Matthew that is read on St. Andrew's day. This saint's day is the first of the liturgical year in the missal, at the beginning of the Christmas cycle. Matthew relates that as Jesus walked by the sea of Galilee, He saw two brothers, Simon, who is called Peter, and Andrew, who had let down their nets into the sea, for they were fishermen; He said to them: "Follow me, and I will make you fishers of men." Though they were

brothers and had begun their apostolic mission together, the Christian liturgy has separated them: St. Peter's day is celebrated with St. Paul's on the 29th of June. The miniature, however, represents the newly elected brothers together as described in the Gospel (Matt. 4 : 18–19). Peter and Andrew have left their boat, symbolic of the life they have forsaken, to kneel at the feet of Christ. They are about to join the other disciples, among whom are already two Apostles with halos. The meeting between the Messiah and His "fishers of men" is shown with much dignity. The noble bearing of the figures, their ample and majestic mantles, and the naturalness of their gestures give to the whole scene a feeling of real grandeur. The brothers, nevertheless, have been painted with the evident intention of representing two bearded and humble fishermen who have come in answer to the call of the Master. The variety of their features, and the accuracy of such details as the position of Andrew's knees and hands, are as rigorously observed as they would have been by a Flemish artist.

The landscape also clearly demonstrates that the Italian artists are accustomed, like northern ones, to draw from life and use the outdoor world as model. The shore by the sea of Galilee with its pebbles, the reeds by the water, the boat by the water's edge, the oarlocks – all these details are not less true to life than those found in Flemish paintings of the same period. On the contrary: the distant horizon and the indented coast line are unmistakably real. If the rocks do look a little unnatural, they are less so than the round boulders decorated with gold glaze found in Flemish miniatures. The general look of the scene is somewhat artificial, perhaps because there is so little expression on the faces, Peter's and Andrew's excepted, but chiefly because of the unpleasantly brilliant coloring. It may be, however, that this unreality is allied with the luminosity which pervades the whole picture, and stands for the true light seen on the shores of Galilee. The greatest merit of this page is its transparency, which throws the details into relief in the most striking manner.

We do not know the artist, but we do know the master illuminator who organized the team of illustrators and decorators working on the Missal. We are fortunate in that he signed his name "Actavantes de Actavantibus" in the frame of two miniatures and specified that he worked between 1485 and 1487. It was not the miniatures that took up so much of his time, for the Missal contains only six of these, but the decoration as a whole. In Flemish workshops, the miniaturists, that is to say, the painters commissioned to illustrate the text, were never in charge of such minor work as, for instance, the initials or line endings, and probably not of the marginal decorations. In Attavante's workshop, a manuscript once written was then completed in all its details. It remains to be seen whether even the transcription itself may not have been done there too; Attavante could thus be called a publisher, in the modern meaning of the word. In any case, the harmony between the miniatures and the minor decorations is nowhere so close as in his workshop. Both crafts were exacting, insofar as talent and skill were concerned. Margins, for instance, were profusely adorned with medallions showing the same personages that appear in the miniatures and painted, moreover, in exactly the same colors. The specialists in these two techniques have an identical style, so that one might easily be led to believe that the same hand was responsible for both, but this would have been a practical impossibility, owing to the superabundant decoration of the Missal. Attavante certainly required the help of a great number of assistants to complete the luxurious ornamentation that is lavished on this eight-hundred-page book. From the point of view of decoration, no other workshop can compare to Attavante's. The best manuscripts executed there display a richness that is beyond imagination, of which the page reproduced here can give but a limited idea. Even so, one regrets the abusive use of harsh reds, blues, and greens in this miniature which, on the fully decorated double pages, is hardly bearable. We meet here another form of art, classic in its dignity but, it must be admitted, not always measured in other respects.

Attavante made this Missal in Florence for Mathias Corvinus, king of Hungary. The exacting taste of this patron, who was a great connoisseur of art, explains the fantastic luxuriousness of this book. The owner had, fortunately for us, directed the publisher to decorate the margins of the Missal with liberal use of his coat of arms and emblems. Later the manuscript passed into Mary of Hungary's library and then to that of Philip II, who ordered a miniaturist to erase systematically all the marks of the original owner. One can still find, however, one or two emblems of the King of Hungary: a raven holding a ring in its beak, and even his motto *Sic fata jubent*, written on a scroll joining the two parts of a broken twig. There are several portraits of Mathias crowned with a laurel wreath, and some also of his wife Mary and of his natural son, that the man charged with altering the marks of ownership did not recognize, and anyway could have erased only with great difficulty. In these many portraits one sees again how painstakingly accurate the Italian artist was; but instead of accentuating some peculiarity of feature, as his Flemish colleague would have done, he was inclined to idealize them. Thus both painters used man and nature as their models, but how differently they saw them!

## 50 The Crowning with Thorns

BOOK OF HOURS OF HENNESSY. *Bruges. About 1540.*
*190 folios ($4^1/_2 \times 3^3/_8$"); 2 small miniatures; 26 large miniatures, each with historiated frame on opposite page.*
*Ms. II 158, ff. 79 v and 80 r*

THE ICONOGRAPHIC CYCLE of the Passion was more popular in Germanic countries than elsewhere. In Holland, for instance, the Hours of Our Lady were not illustrated with the eight scenes of the life of the Virgin, or the childhood of Jesus, which they may also use, but with eight miniatures depicting the great moments of the Passion. Under French influence, some of the Dutch books of hours have combined the two cycles and thus present sixteen scenes, distributed most often in the form of eight miniatures and eight initials. In the southern Netherlands, particularly in Bruges, books of hours are even found with eight miniatures, each divided into two compartments, in which the two cycles are represented one above the other. This illustration representing the Crowning with Thorns is placed at Tierce in the Hours of Our Lady, and shows that the scenes of the Passion of Christ have, once and for all, replaced the story of the Virgin – even the composite one encountered in numerous Bruges manuscripts until the mid-sixteenth century.

As is customary in prayer books, the subject of the miniature is drawn from the Gospels. This does not mean, of course, that the miniaturist had to consult Matthew 27 : 27–29 in order to follow the sacred text in every detail. An important iconographic tradition existed, and he could also find inspiration in the theatrical representations of mysteries and passions that kept alive,

Ad terciam. Aue maria. &c.
DEUS in adiu
torium me
um inten
de.
Domi
ne ad adiuuandum me
festina.
Gloria patri et filio et
spiritui sancto.
Sicut erat in principi
o et nunc et semper et in secla
seculorum amen. Alleluia.

and sometimes even enriched, the readings of the Gospels. No wonder, then, that so poignant a scene as the mocking of Christ is rendered with such realism and even coarseness. Matthew writes that Christ, after He had been scourged, was delivered by Pilate to the people to be crucified; the rods and the whip are still at the feet of Christ, whose whole body bleeds from the wounds; a pool of blood is spreading over the tile floor. The evangelist continues: "Then the soldiers of the governor took Jesus into the common hall, and gathered unto him the whole band of soldiers. And they stripped him, and put on him a scarlet robe. And when they had platted a crown of thorns, they put it upon his head, and a reed in his right hand: and they bowed the knee before him, and mocked him, saying, Hail, King of the Jews!" The painter illustrates further torments not included in the description of the evangelist. A man with the face of a brute presents Christ with a cat-tail, while his companions-in-arms delight in inflicting more pain on their victim. The miniaturist has rendered this torture very boldly entangled gestures. The head of Christ is caught as in a vice between two sticks which squeeze the skull and the chin, forcing the crown of thorns into the flesh. This torment, which is an addition to those described in the sacred text, was, however, not invented by the painter. Tortures of this kind had already been represented in German manuscripts of the fourteenth century, which had an iconographic tradition for the crown of thorns pressed into the flesh by means of two big sticks set in the form of a cross. It was, however, in Holland that this tradition most often recurred, for instance in the Hours of Mary van Vronensteyn (plate 37). But in this present case, the Flemish painter, inspired by Dutch tradition, far exceeds his model. Indeed, the artist has given the tormentors the most brutal features, the most sadistic grins. In contrast, those of the procurators have been endowed with a superb demeanor as they come to look at their victim. The accompanying soldiers have the faces of peasants. Nevertheless, in this lively, brightly colored little scene it is Christ who commands attention. Christ is shown lacerated and bleeding to this extent in few easel paintings, and their colors have faded; in this miniature, however, the colors have retained their original freshness. We can well understand why the painter could not use scarlet for Christ's clothing, as the Gospel describes, for such a color would have detracted from the many traces of blood. The frame of the left page is architectural and tends to make the picture look like one wing of a large altarpiece. In the development of marginal decoration, this is the last stage adopted by the Flemish miniaturists before they learned to content themselves with a simple frame, similar to those of easel paintings. The impression of depth is so skillfully done that the statues, as well as the brackets on which they are standing, look like real carvings. The two figures painted in grisaille against a gold background are presumably two of the prophets who announced the Passion of Christ. The lower frieze continues, like a predella, the principal subject, and leads the spectator toward the next scene of the Passion: Christ carrying the Cross.

The right page shows a decoration which is in every way different from the subject described above. This hunting scene, with its peaceful atmosphere and soft coloring, is soothing after the cruel tortures in the left-hand picture. It is probable, however, that the two subjects are connected; the poor stag, harassed from all sides by dogs in the stream and hunters on the bank, may symbolize Christ, likewise fallen into the hands of His enemies and doomed to perish.

This page, though its mood is so different, is as perfect as the other from the pictorial point of view. The meadows vanishing into the sky line, the bushy thickets, the transparent water rippled by the dogs, the graceful tree, all are rendered with a sense of reality never found before in such a variety of effects. The *Chroniques de Hainaut* (plate 27), the Hours of Vronensteyn (plate 37), Chevrot's *City of God* (plate 26), the Pontifical of Sens (plate 38), to quote only a few, have already enchanted us with their perfect portraits, landscapes, perspectives, and other details; but in this double page, the painter has tried his hand in all of these aspects at once, as if he wanted to give us samples of his multiple talents, and in each he is entirely successful.

The stylistic and pictorial innovations already pointed out in the Hours of Philip of Cleves (plate 48) soon degenerated into a type of illumination which is quite pleasant, though unfortunately lifeless. This new mannerism provoked the reaction that is clearly manifested in such works as the Hours of Hennessy. The reaction against mawkish color, sweet faces, and too-elaborate composition explain the name "neo-realism" given to this movement. This style could not have developed without the progress made by the previous generation. Simon Bening was probably one of the most important of those responsible for the new trend in Flemish painting, and Bruges seems to have been the center from which the most successful productions of this new artistic current were issued. In the books painted in the manner of the Hours of Hennessy, some views of Bruges usually decorate the miniatures. Though such a profusely adorned manuscript is necessarily the work of many collaborators, this Christ with the Crown of Thorns can be ascribed to Simon Bening himself, for no page is more worthy of this truly exceptional illuminator.

In this double page, the Italian Renaissance has left only a few traces of its influence: the style, for instance, of the columns of the great hall and the arcades they support. It is a work still almost entirely Gothic in spirit that impresses us with such perfection. Flemish illumination reached its peak at the very moment it was about to give way forever to the printed book and to engraving. Moreover, the miniature has lost its original character and is now about to withdraw from the book, for it has become an ordinary small painting. The miniature on the right of this folio, indeed, is like a canvas or a panel painting, duly surrounded by a frame and partly hidden by the text. This was done in accordance with a decorative conception, the significance of which has been explained (plate 48). In other countries, the art of illumination was less perfected, and remained in the province of book illustration. It had besides, as early as the end of the fifteenth century, ceased to be of importance. The production in Bruges asserts itself as an exception within the history of art, and disappears at the moment it reaches the summit of its splendor.

THE SELECTION of the best manuscripts from the ancient "Library of Burgundy" has given us the opportunity to admire the art of illustrating manuscripts in western Europe from the beginning to the consummation, as well as intermediary developments. It happens that the first and last pictures in this book, after we have followed the evolution of illumination during the Middle Ages, prove to have something in common. Starting with a Roman miniature, or a faithful copy of a Roman work impregnated with the classical humanism of that cultured epoch, we witness the slow rise of art in a new world that strives to find its own forms of expression in the domain of pictures. During the Gothic period some localized styles asserted themselves, more or less rapidly and more or less successfully. In Flanders, thanks to various influences from the North and the South, a typical style evolved that was slow to discover its own values, being constantly hampered by mannerisms. The Hours of Hennessy may be considered one of the manuscripts that expresses this high level of achievement at its best – for it was an achievement! This is why, when speaking of style in connection with this work, we may also speak of humanism – not classical humanism, but a more individualistic and in certain aspects a more crude humanism, here unfolds its multiple splendors, without ostentation or false modesty, to our admiring gaze.